HOW TO PASS

DIAGRAMMATIC
REASONING TESTS

HOW TO PASS

DIAGRAMMATIC REASONING TESTS

Essential practice for abstract, input type
and spatial reasoning tests

MIKE BRYON

KOGAN
PAGE

London and Philadelphia

Publisher's note
Every possible effort has been made to ensure that the information contained in this book is accurate at the time of going to press, and the publishers and author cannot accept responsibility for any errors or omissions, however caused. No responsibility for loss or damage occasioned to any person acting, or refraining from action, as a result of the material in this publication can be accepted by the editor, the publisher or the author.

First published in Great Britain and the United States in 2008 by Kogan Page Limited

120 Pentonville Road
London N1 9JN
United Kingdom
www.koganpage.com

525 South 4th Street, #241
Philadelphia PA 19147
USA

© Mike Bryon, 2008

The right of Mike Bryon to be identified as the author of this work has been asserted by him in accordance with the Copyright, Designs and Patents Act 1988.

ISBN 978 0 7494 4971 1

British Library Cataloguing-in-Publication Data

A CIP record for this book is available from the British Library.

Library of Congress Cataloging-in-Publication Data

Bryon, Mike.
  How to pass diagrammatic reasoning tests : essential practice for abstract, input type and spacial reasoning tests / Mike Bryon.
      p. cm.
  ISBN 978-0-7494-4971-1
  1. Reasoning (Psychology)--Testing. I. Title.
  BF442.B79 2008
  153.4'3--dc22
                                   2008027145

Typeset by Saxon Graphics Ltd, Derby
Printed and bound in India by Replika Press Pvt Ltd

Contents

Acknowledgements

I owe thanks to Anabel Gelhaar and Andrea Zigon for devising and drawing the conceptual/spatial reasoning questions in Chapter 4.

A unique source of essential practice

Diagrammatic reasoning tests involve a series of pictorial or diagrammatic questions with little or no resort to words or numbers. Some require you to undertake highly complex transformations or manipulations of awkward shapes all in your head against a tight timescale (see Chapter 4). Others involve shapes or letters that apply rules. You may have to reverse a sequence of letters or shapes, or drop or add letters or shapes, and so on. Again you must complete these tasks against a tight time constraint (see Chapter 3). Another style of question requires you to identify features in common to complete a series or choose an answer that correctly completes a series of shapes from a number of suggestions (see Chapter 2). You will not find another book that provides practice for all three of these, the most common types of diagrammatic reasoning tests.

If you have to pass a diagrammatic reasoning test or never seem to do well in them, if you have been searching for a source of practice or have found it hard to get sufficient practice material, then this is the book for you. You can learn to master these common assessments and become more confident and accurate in every sort of diagrammatic reasoning test. This book provides everything you need for a successful programme of revision or review and for many candidates will mean the difference between pass and fail. It contains over 300 practice questions, with answers and explanations and advice on how to show your true potential. You will not find another book on this subject with so many practice questions. Uniquely it also offers 26 timed mini-tests so you can develop the all-important speed at answering these questions and approach a real test with a new confidence.

Tests of diagrammatic reasoning feature in the recruitment process for many positions, including for example professional services, finance, accountancy, graduate traineeships, architecture, engineering and even the UKCAT (the test you must pass in order to win a place at medical school). Such a test is likely to be one of a number of sub-tests that make up the assessment. Commonly the assessment will include a test of verbal and numerical reasoning as well as a test of diagrammatic reasoning. You take these sub-tests one after the other, online at a computer or with paper and pen. It is important that you realize that you are likely to be one of a large number of candidates, and you must achieve a score better than the majority in order to pass through to the next stage in the recruitment process. You may also have to achieve a well-balanced score across a number of sub-tests.

Doing well in these common assessments is largely down to practice of the right sort, the right amount, at the right time. Success in any psychometric test often requires hard work, time and commitment. The choice is entirely yours. If you rise to the challenge, your dream career could become a reality. The alternative is to risk failure.

Start by getting test wise

It is really important that you understand exactly what the test you face involves. You will be astonished at how many people attend a test not knowing what to expect. The first time they learn of the type of questions involved is when the test administrator describes them just before the test begins. Don't make this mistake. You need to know the nature of the challenge as soon as possible.

The organization to which you have applied should have sent you a description of the type of questions and the format with the letter or e-mail of invitation. If they have not done this then have a look on their website or contact them and ask them to describe the test. Be sure to get details on:

- how many sub-tests the test battery comprises;
- what the title of each sub-test is;
- what sort of question makes up a sub-test (you should be provided with, or directed to, a description of each type of question);
- how many questions each sub-test includes;
- how long you have to complete each sub-test;
- whether it is multiple-choice or short-answer;
- whether you complete it with pen and paper or at a computer terminal;
- if you face a numeracy test, whether or not a calculator is allowed.

Adopt a winning mindset

It is common to experience feelings of irritation or resentment about having to sit a test. It is crucial that you put these feeling aside. They can be very counterproductive. Try not to wonder about the validity of the test. What you think of it and its predictive value is entirely irrelevant. You need to do well in this test if you are to realize your goal. Focus on only that goal and for a few weeks put all else aside. You really need to let your determination to do well take over your life for a while.

Some very clever and highly educated people do not do well at these tests. In some cases their training and inclination do not serve them well under the rather artificial conditions of a timed test. This happens when, for example, the candidate thinks too deeply about the question or studies the questions too carefully. Some place too high an emphasis on accuracy at the expense of speed. The outcome is that their test result does not reflect their true ability or their achievements to date. If you are such a person, remember that being too careful or thinking deeply may put you at a considerable disadvantage. For the sake of greater speed you may need to develop an approach that involves a slightly greater risk of getting a question wrong. Work hard on your exam technique and do not rest until you can demonstrate the necessary balance between speed and accuracy. Practice is key to achieving this. Make sure you allow yourself lots of time to develop a winning approach.

Doing well in a test is not simply a matter of intelligence. It is critical that you realize that, to do well, you have to try hard too. Over some weeks before the test you will need to undertake a programme of review, and during the exam you will need to really 'go for it'. After the exam you should feel mentally fatigued. If you don't then you probably failed to apply yourself sufficiently and may not have fully done yourself justice.

Devise and implement an unbeatable study plan

High-scoring candidates in every exam are confident of their abilities. They know what to expect and find the exam contains few if any surprises. They turn up at the test centre looking forward to the opportunity to demonstrate how good they really have become and are able to demonstrate a highly effective exam technique. To make sure you are such a candidate, begin by preparing a study plan well in advance of the test date.

Step 1 Know what to expect

The first thing to do is to make sure that you know exactly what to expect at each stage of the test. This should include the exact nature of each task and how long you are allowed. If the test is online or administered at a computer screen it is important that you are familiar with the screen icons and format, so that you can concentrate on the questions.

Step 2 Make an honest assessment of your strengths and weaknesses

To prepare thoroughly for any assessment you should concentrate your efforts on the areas in which you are weakest. You probably already know which part of the assessment you would fail, were you to take the test tomorrow. But you really need to try to go a step further than this and assess the extent to which your area(s) of personal challenge may let you down. Only then can you ensure that you spend sufficient time addressing the challenge. You should repeat such an assessment at a number of points throughout your programme of revision. You can then observe your progress and focus on the area(s) that continue to represent a risk of failure.

To obtain a good indication of the extent of the challenge you face, select three or four examples of each style of question broadly representative of the level of difficulty found in the real assessment. You could use questions from this or any other Kogan Page practice book. Attempt these questions under exam-type conditions and score them. It is then a simple matter of concentrating on the parts of the test in which you did least well. Remember to repeat this exercise throughout your programme of revision.

Step 3 Plan a programme of practice

Now you need to decide how much time to spend preparing for the challenge. The sooner you start the better, and a little but often is better than occasional long sessions. The assessment that you undertook in Step 2 should allow you to decide how much of a challenge the test represents. Take it seriously and avoid the trap of promising yourself that you will start tomorrow. For some candidates tomorrow never comes, or it comes far too late. A winning plan is likely to involve work over a minimum of two weeks, spending a couple of hours revising three times a week.

Step 4 Obtain every bit of free material and then buy more

Many candidates facing psychometric tests cannot find sufficient relevant practice material. Some is available free of charge from, for example, your university careers department, as downloads on the internet or borrowed from libraries. More can be obtained either through subscription websites or through books. You will almost certainly need to use this purchased material in addition to that which is freely available. You will find over 200 more diagrammatic reasoning questions in my *Ultimate Psychometric Tests* (published by Kogan Page).

If you also face verbal and numerical tests then you can practise on full-length practice tests at www.shl.com and www.psl.co.uk. You have to register. Free downloads are available at www.mike bryon.com, and at this site there is no requirement to register. In the Kogan Page testing series you will find these intermediate-level books:

- *The Verbal Reasoning Test Workbook* (contains 700 practice questions);
- *The Numeracy Test Workbook* (also contains 700 questions);
- *The Ultimate Psychometric Tests* (contains over 1,000 questions).

You will also find these advanced-level books:

- *How to Pass Advanced Verbal Reasoning Tests*;
- *How to Pass Advanced Numeracy Tests*;
- *How to Pass Graduate Psychometric Tests*;
- *The Graduate Psychometric Test Workbook*.

You can order these books at 20 per cent discount at www.mike bryon.com.

Step 5 Undertake two sorts of practice

First and to get the most from your practice, begin working in a relaxed situation without constraint of time, reviewing questions and working out the answers. Feel free to review the answers and explanations in Chapter 5 as much as you wish. Chapters 2, 3 and 4 all begin with a block of practice questions dedicated to undertaking this sort of warm-up practice.

Once you are familiar with the challenge of each question type then you should start to practise under realistic test conditions. This involves working against the clock without help or interruption. The purpose is to develop a good exam technique and to learn not to spend too long on any one question and practise at educated guessing. The 26 mini-tests found in this volume are perfect for this second sort of practice. Use them to make sure you will get off to a really good start in a real diagrammatic reasoning test. For a real test experience be sure to attempt them under realistic test conditions and set yourself the challenge of getting all five questions right.

To get the most out of this sort of practice, set yourself the personal challenge of trying to beat or match your last score each time you take a mini-test.

Answers and explanation to all the practice questions are found in Chapter 5.

What to expect on the day

You may have to complete a test online (at home) or you may be invited to attend a training or recruitment centre to take the test. In some cases you have to take two tests: the first online and, if you pass, another at an assessment centre. All this detail will be included in your letter or e-mail of invitation, so read it carefully.

Remember, the candidates who do best are not usually the ones who are fearful or who feel resentment about having to take a test. Look forward to the challenge and the opportunity it represents. You are there to demonstrate your abilities and prove to the organization that you are a suitable candidate. The best candidates approach the test with confidence in themselves and their abilities. This should not discourage you. Everyone can develop this approach. The secret is preparation. Attend the test fully prepared for the challenge and use it to demonstrate how good you have become.

Turn up fully prepared, having spent many hours practising for the test, ready to take full advantage of your strengths and having addressed any areas of weakness. Do not underestimate how long it can take to prepare for a test. Start as soon as you receive notice that you must attend.

It is obviously really important that you listen carefully to the instructions provided before a test begins. But appreciate the fact that you may well be feeling nervous and this may affect your concentration, so make yourself focus on what is being said. Much of the information will be a repeat of the test description sent to you with the letter inviting you to the test. So read and reread this document before the day of the test.

Pay particular attention to instructions on how many questions there are in each sub-test, and be sure you are familiar with the demands of each style of question. Check for instructions to turn over the page. You will be surprised how many people reach the bottom of a page and wrongly conclude that they have reached the end of the questions. Such people stop working and wait when they should be working away at the remaining questions.

Keep track of the time during the test and manage how long you spend on any one question. You must keep going right up to the end. Aim to get the balance between speed and accuracy right. Try to attempt every question, even if you risk getting some wrong. Practice can really help develop this skill.

If you hit a difficult section of questions don't lose heart. Keep going – everyone gets some questions wrong. You may find that you excel at the next set of questions.

Aim to make a really good start and to keep going

In every test every question counts, but try especially hard to get the first question right, then the first five questions and then all the rest!

Make sure you use the really useful mini-tests at the end of each chapter of questions to practise making a really good start. They take only a few minutes so can be fitted into even the busiest schedule.

Guessing can pay

If you do not know the answer to a question you have little alternative but to guess. In a multiple-choice test, straight guessing offers perhaps a 20 per cent chance of guessing correctly (assuming there are five suggested answers from which to choose). You can improve on this if you know that some of the suggested answers are wrong. You can rule them out and increase your chances of guessing correctly. Guessing plays an important part in many candidates' test-taking strategy, especially in the later part of each sub-test when time may be running out.

If you suffer a disability

If your ability to undertake any test could be adversely affected by a disability then speak to the organization to which you are applying and seek their advice on how your requirements can best be accommodated. Provide full details of your condition and be clear about the special arrangements you require. You may be allowed extra time, or a test reader, or someone to record your answers. Braille or large-text versions of the test may be made available.

It is reasonable to expect that your requirements will be given proper consideration and accommodated when possible. Evidence of your condition may be required. Be sure to raise your needs at an early stage so that the organizers have time to accommodate your needs. It will also give you sufficient time to obtain any formal proof of your condition that may be required.

How to use this book

Each chapter starts with a large block of warm-up questions and concludes with mini-tests. Use the block of practice questions to become familiar with the challenge and the mini-tests to practise under exam-like conditions. Just as in a real test, the questions get progressively harder. Answers and explanations are found in Chapter 5.

To get the most out of your practice and to help make it feel more realistic, set yourself the challenge of trying to beat your own score each time you take a mini-test. You will have to try hard and take the challenge seriously.

Record of mini-test scores

Don't stop practising until you consistently score 5 out of 5 in these mini-tests!

Mini-test 1: Score:

Mini-test 2: Score:

Mini-test 3: Score:

Mini-test 4: Score:

Mini-test 5: Score:

Copy the answer sheet to ensure that you can record your score in all 26 mini-tests contained in this volume.

What to do if you fail

If you are reading this book having failed a diagrammatic reasoning test and this has prevented you from realizing a career goal, then take heart. It is entirely normal for candidates to fail the more popular tests on the first few attempts. It certainly does not mean that you do not have the ability to do the job or course in question. However, it does mean that you need to improve on your performance in the test used to recruit to that position.

Failure does not mean that the company will not welcome a future application from you. Should you be successful at a later stage, once you are employed you will be judged by your performance in the job, not your past test scores. It will not impinge on your future career prospects within the organization.

It is likely that over half the candidates who sit a psychometric test will fail. If this happens to you then ask the organization to provide you with feedback on your score and identify the parts of the test that you had problems with. Recall and note down the types of question, how many there were and the level of difficulty. Be honest with yourself and try to assess what it is that you need to do in order to pass the next time.

I know candidates who repeatedly failed a test. They eventually managed to pass after setting about a major programme of revision. Others simply needed to get more used to the test and working in a timed exam-type situation. Remember, it is not uncommon for accomplished applicants to fail a test because they thought too long or too deeply about the questions. Their work or studies did not prepare them for a test in which you have to act very quickly to complete all the questions in the given time.

In order to succeed, plan a programme of revision and improvement, concentrating on what you are least good at. Seek out sufficient practice material and get down to some seriously hard work.

Apply again as soon as you are able, fully prepared and confident in your abilities.

It will take courage and determination to try again and keep working to improve yourself until you pass, but these are qualities of which you can be proud. With the right approach you will address your personal challenges and go on to pass. You will then be able to look back on what you can regard as a significant achievement.

May I take this opportunity to wish you every success in the psychometric test that you face. If you encounter a test that contains questions of a type not covered by this book or the suggested further reading mentioned earlier, then by all means e-mail me at help@mikebryon.com and I will hopefully be able to let you know of a suitable source of practice.

Abstract reasoning tests

SHL Ltd is a leading publisher of psychometric assessments. Its 'inductive reasoning test' measures the ability to think conceptually and analytically. If you face this test or one of the very many others like it, then use the practice tests here to become completely familiar with the key challenges. You will see a dramatic improvement in your likely score.

This chapter comprises 105 abstract reasoning practice questions, which are organized into a block of 85 practice questions and then four mini-tests. In total, there are four styles of abstract question. The first requires you to identify a quality that is common to two shapes. You have to select which of the three suggested answers also possesses the quality. The second and third styles require that you complete a series by identifying which of the suggested answers should be placed in the empty space. The fourth and final style of question asks you to identify the correct code for a new shape from the codes given for the example shapes.

You will be prepared for any type of abstract reasoning test if you practise all four styles of question covered here. The type of questions in this book may differ from those found in the assessment you face, but they all examine your command of the same key principles. The main ones are: rotation – where a shape is turned; alteration – where a shape changes into something else and is then changed back; consistency – where a change is made to a shape and is then consistently applied; replacement – where a shape or shapes are replaced by others; attention to detail – where you simply have to look carefully at the diagrams. These principles are really not as complex as they sound and will become clearer once you get practising. As in a real test, the questions in this chapter are easy at first and then get progressively harder.

Style one

Identify a quality that the two shapes have in common. Select which of the three suggested answers also possesses the quality.

Q1.

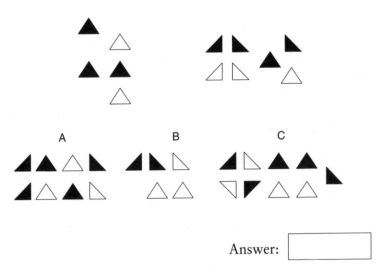

Answer:

Q2.

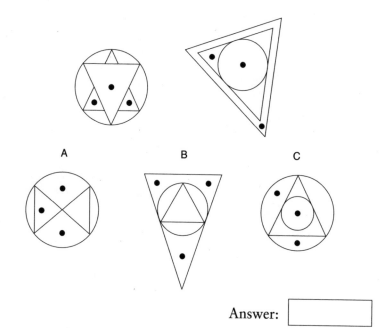

A   B   C

Answer: [   ]

Q3.

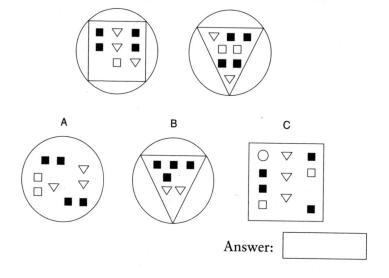

A   B   C

Answer: [   ]

Q4.

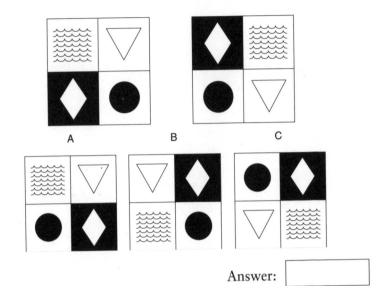

Answer: [   ]

Q5.

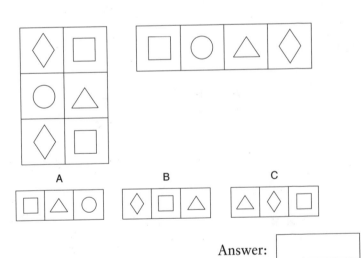

Answer: [   ]

Q6.

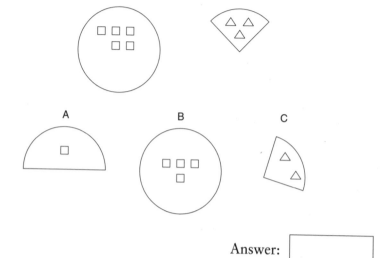

Answer: [ ]

Q7.

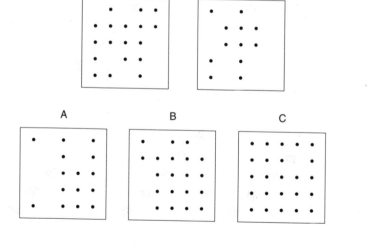

Answer: [ ]

Q8.

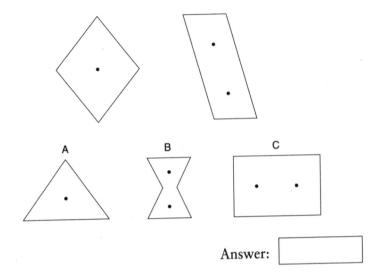

Answer:

Q9.

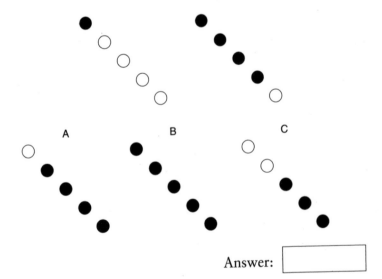

Answer:

Q10.

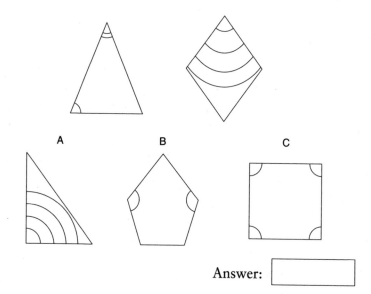

A   B   C

Answer: _____

Style two

This is the second style of abstract reasoning question, which requires you to complete a series or sequence of shapes by identifying which of the suggested answers should be placed in the empty space. Once again these questions test your ability to recognize: rotation – where a shape is turned; alteration – where a shape changes into something else and is then changed back; consistency – where a change is made to a shape and is then consistently applied; replacement – where a shape or shapes are replaced by others; and attention to detail – where you simply have to look carefully at the diagrams.

Q11.

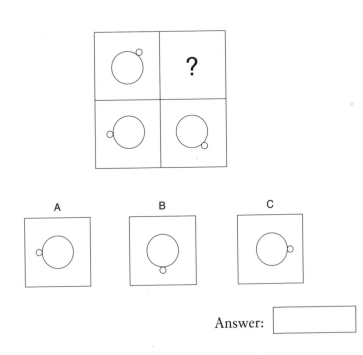

Answer:

Q12.

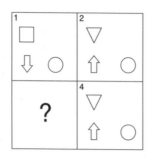

A   B   C

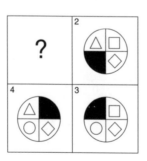

Answer: [   ]

Q13.

A   B   C

Answer: [   ]

Q14.

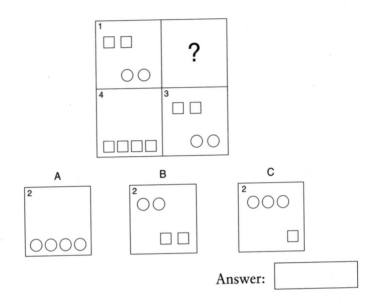

Answer: [   ]

Q15.

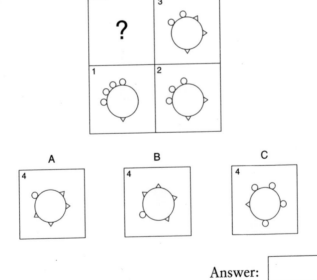

Answer: [   ]

Q16.

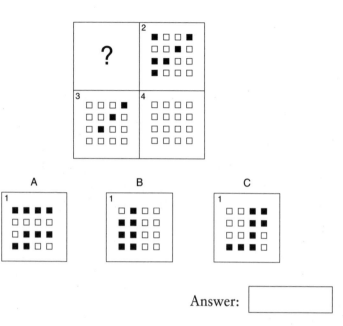

Answer: [   ]

Q17.

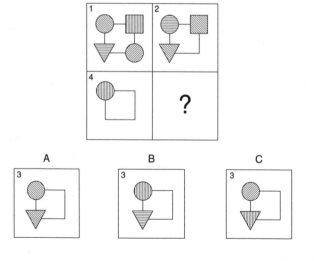

Answer: [   ]

Q18.

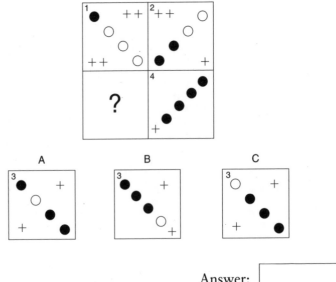

A   B   C

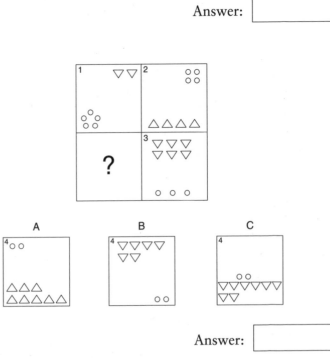

Answer:

Q19.

Answer:

Q20.

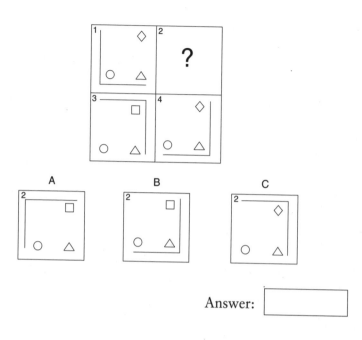

Answer:

Q21.

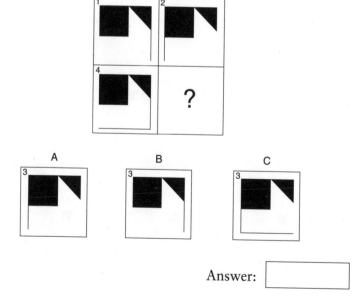

Answer:

Q22.

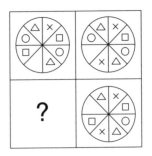

A   B   C

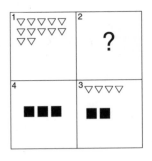

Answer: ⬚

Q23.

A   B   C

Answer: ⬚

Q24.

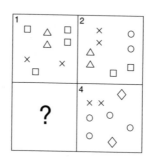

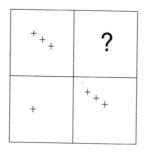

A

B

C

Answer: [   ]

Q25.

A

B

C

Answer: [   ]

Q26.

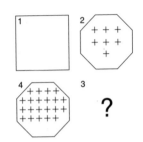

A	B	C	D

Answer: [   ]

Q27.

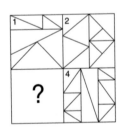

A	B	C

Answer: [   ]

Q28.

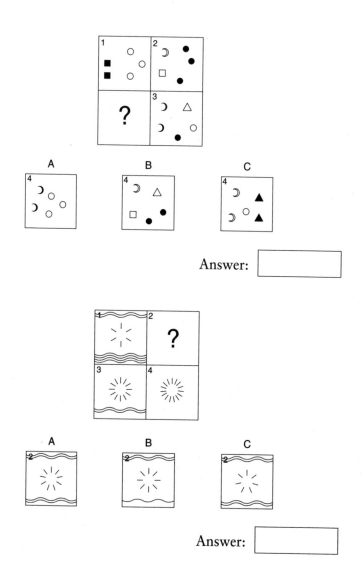

Answer:

Q29.

Answer:

Q30.

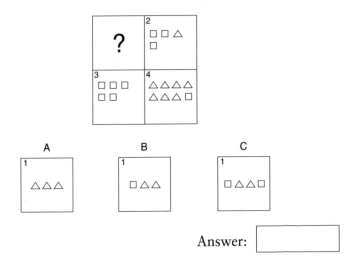

Answer:

Q31.

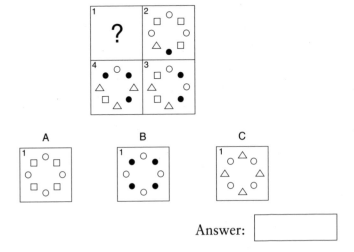

Answer:

Q32.

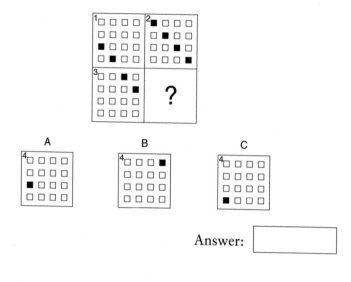

Answer:

Q33.

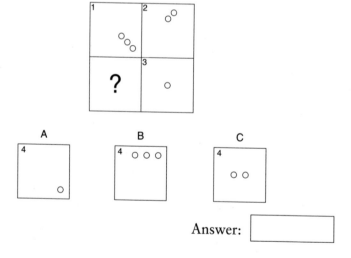

Answer:

Q34.

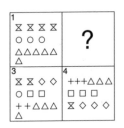

A	B	C

Answer: [   ]

Q35.

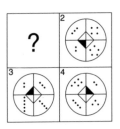

A   B   C

Answer: [   ]

Style three

The third style of question is very similar to the last. It requires you to identify the shape that correctly completes the series. This style of question is very common and used in some of the most widespread abstract reasoning tests. It is important that you realize that the real tests often have very tight time constraints. Candidates often complain that they are unable to answer all the questions in the time allowed. For this reason you may wish to set yourself a bit more of a challenge and attempt this section against the clock. There are 25 questions. Allow yourself just 30 seconds a question. Once you have tried this go back over the questions and look again at any you skipped or did not have time to attempt.

Q36.

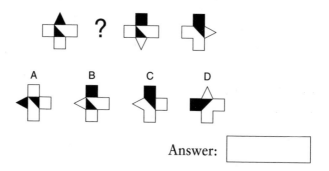

Answer:

Q37.

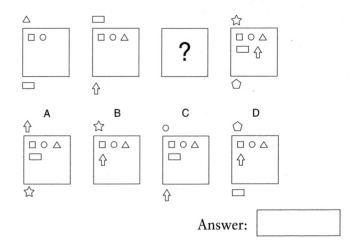

Answer: [   ]

Q38.

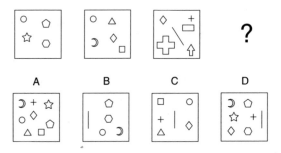

Answer: [   ]

Q39.

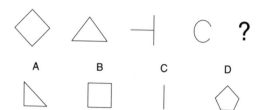

A   B   C   D

Answer: [   ]

Q40.

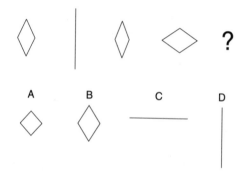

A   B   C   D

Answer: [   ]

Q41.

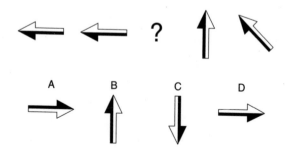

A   B   C   D

Answer: [   ]

Q42.

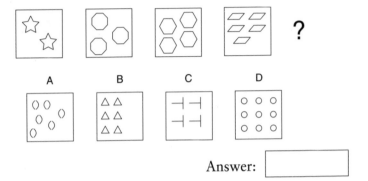

Answer: [   ]

Q43.

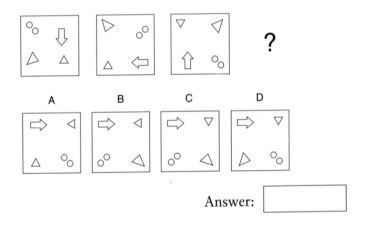

Answer: [   ]

Q44.

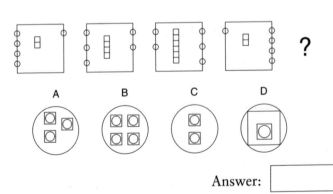

Answer: [   ]

Q45.

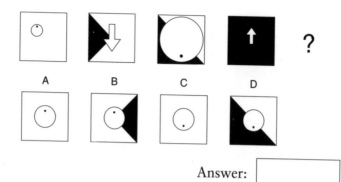

Answer:

Q46.

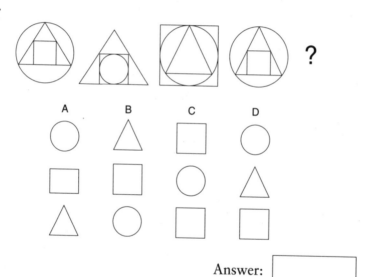

Answer:

Q47.

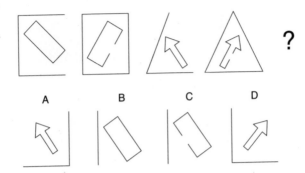

A   B   C   D

Answer: [   ]

Q48.

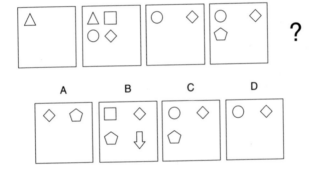

A   B   C   D

Answer: [   ]

Q49.

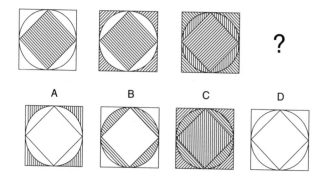

Answer:

Q50.

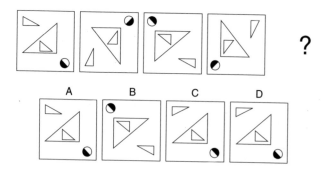

Answer:

Q51.

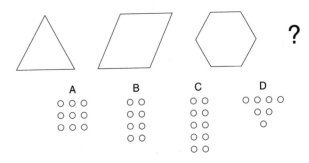

Answer: [   ]

Q52.

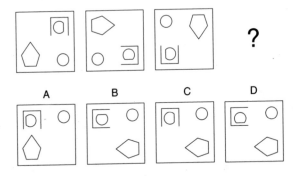

Answer: [   ]

Q53.

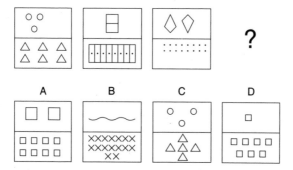

A   B   C   D

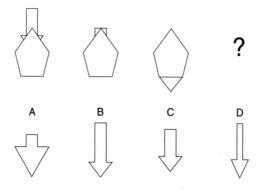

Answer: [   ]

Q54.

A   B   C   D

Answer: [   ]

Q55.

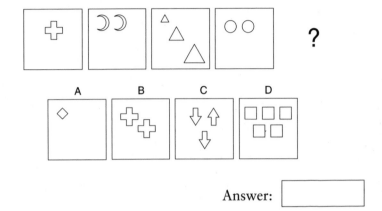

Answer: [   ]

Q56.

Answer: [   ]

Q57.

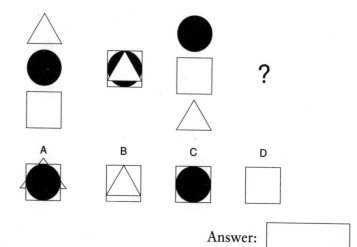

Answer: [   ]

Q58.

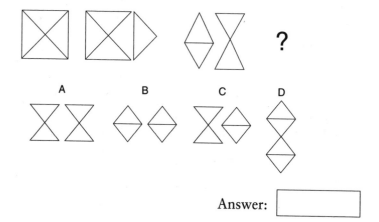

Answer: [   ]

Q59.

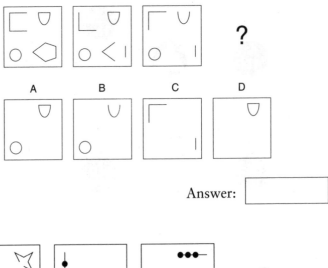

Answer:

Q60.

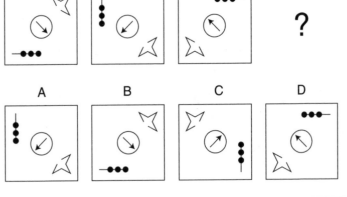

Answer:

Style four

In the fourth style of question your task is to identify the correct code for a new shape from the codes given in the examples. Note that in some instances your answer is restricted to choosing from the suggested answers.

Q61.

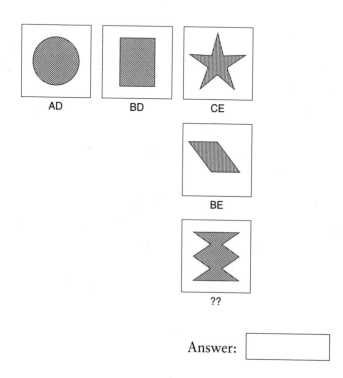

AD   BD   CE

BE

??

Answer: _____

Q62.

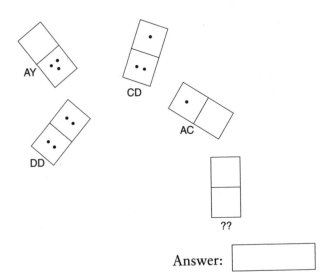

Answer: [   ]

Q63.

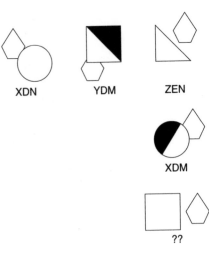

Answer: [   ]

Q64.

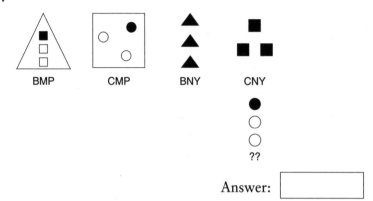

BMP   CMP   BNY   CNY

??

Answer: [   ]

Q65.

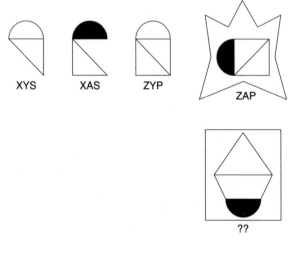

XYS   XAS   ZYP

ZAP

??

Answer: [   ]

Q66.

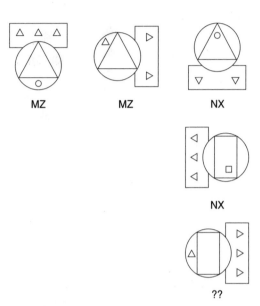

MZ   MZ   NX

NX

??

Answer: [   ]

Q67.

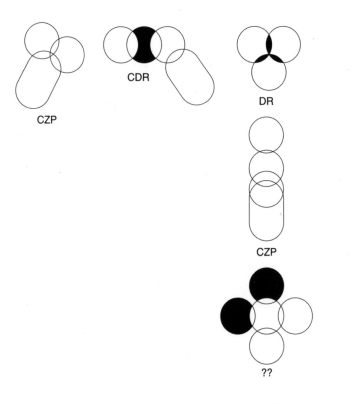

CZP

CDR

DR

CZP

??

Answer: [   ]

Q68.

PR   PR   DE   DE

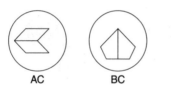

??

Answer:

Q69.

AC   BC   AD

BD

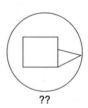

??

Answer:

Q70.

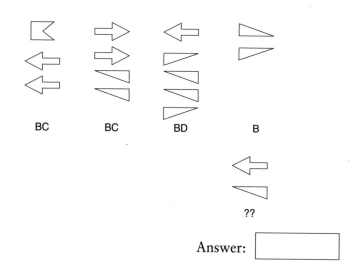

BC   BC   BD   B

??

Answer: [   ]

Q71.

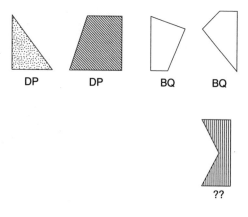

DP   DP   BQ   BQ

??

Answer: [   ]

Q72. Select the most fitting code from the suggested answers.

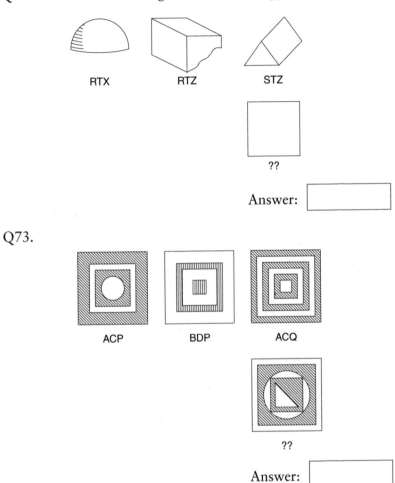

RTX   RTZ   STZ

??

Answer:

Q73.

ACP   BDP   ACQ

??

Answer:

Q74.

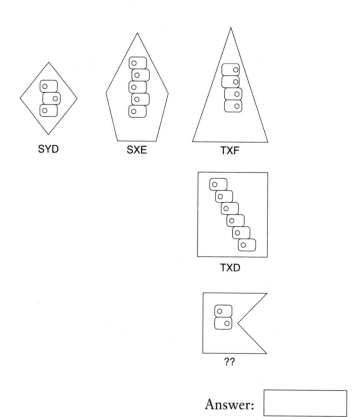

SYD   SXE   TXF

TXD

??

Answer:

Q75.

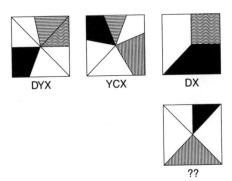

DYX   YCX   DX

??

Answer: [   ]

Q76.

PR   PM   QR   QM

??

Answer: [   ]

Q77.

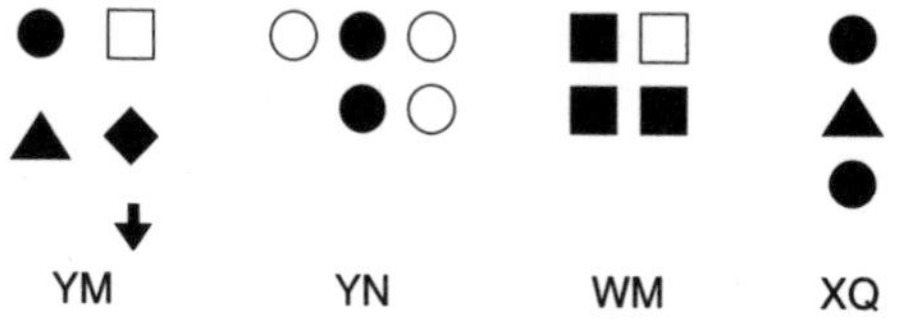
YM
YN
WM
XQ

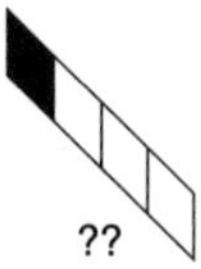
??

Answer:

Q78.

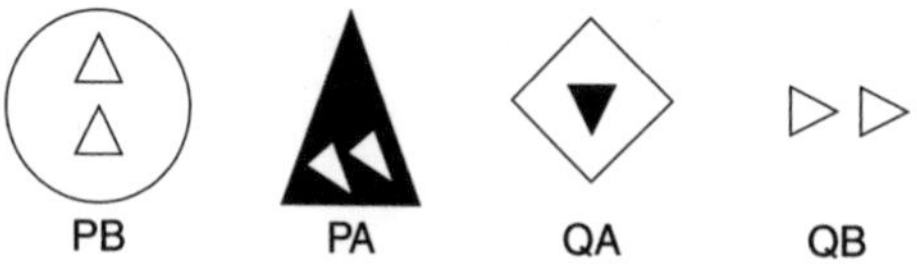
PB
PA
QA
QB

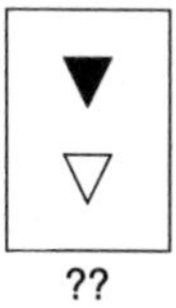
??

Answer:

Q79.

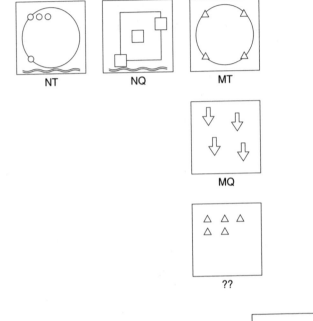

Answer: [   ]

Q80. Select from the suggested answers the most fitting code for the question shape.

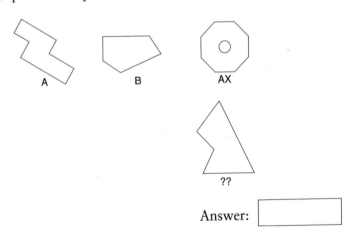

Answer: [   ]

Q81.

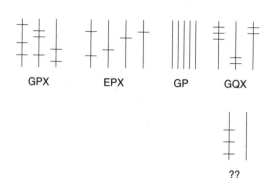

GPX   EPX   GP   GQX

??

Answer:

Q82.

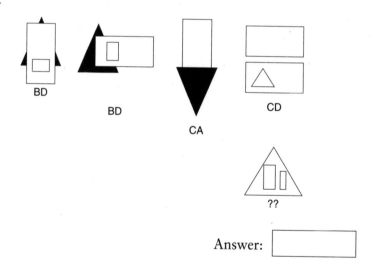

BD

BD

CA

CD

??

Answer:

Q83.

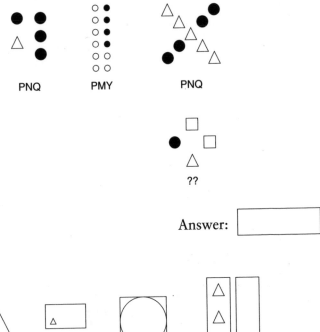

PNQ   PMY   PNQ

??

Answer:

Q84.

PF   PD   QD   PE

??

Answer:

Q85.

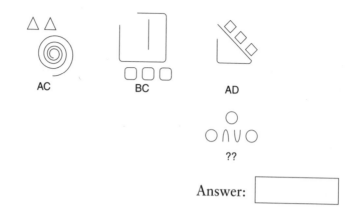

AC

BC

AD

??

Answer:

Four mini-tests

Each of the following practice mini-tests contains five multiple-choice questions. The first is of average difficulty, and they become progressively harder. This is exactly what would happen in the real test that you face. Set yourself the time limit of seven minutes in which to complete each practice mini-test.

Study each question carefully. Select your answer from the suggested answers or codes and write the corresponding letter or code in the answer box. Then move on to the next question.

Answers and explanation to these practice mini-test questions are found in Chapter 5.

Don't turn the page until you are ready to begin the first mini-test.

Mini-test 1

Identify the quality in common.

Q1.

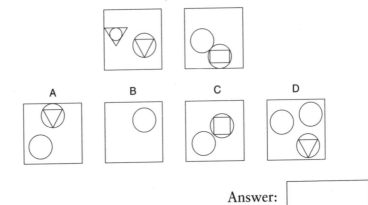

Answer:

Q2.

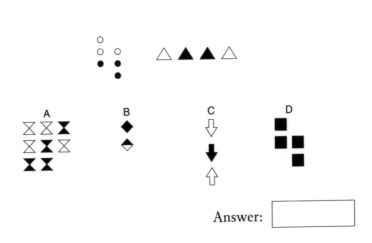

Answer:

Q3.

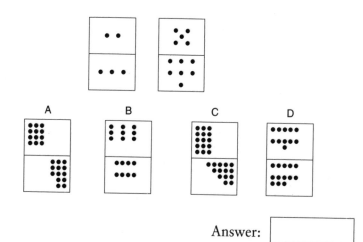

Answer: [   ]

Q4.

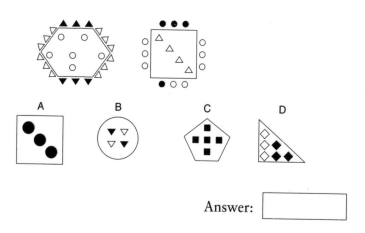

Answer: [   ]

Q5.

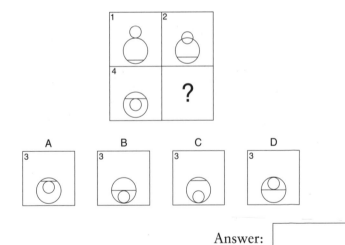

Answer: [   ]

End of test

Mini-test 2

Complete the series.

Q1.

Answer: [   ]

Q2.

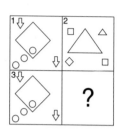

A	B	C	D
	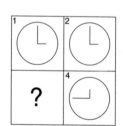		

Answer:

Q3.

1	2
?	4

A	B	C	D

Answer:

Q4.

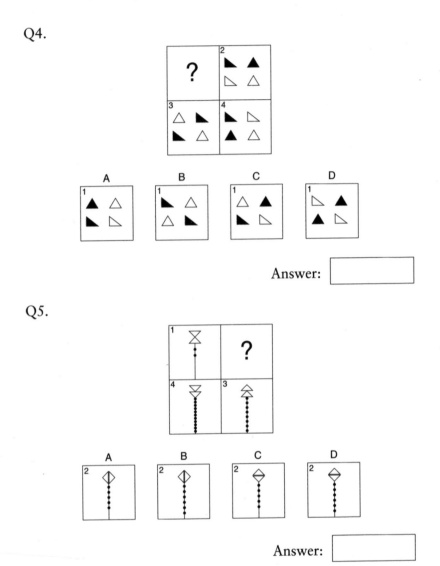

Answer:

Q5.

Answer:

End of test

Mini-test 3

Complete the sequence.

Q1.

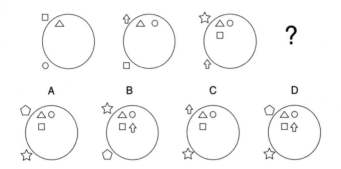

Answer: [   ]

Q2.

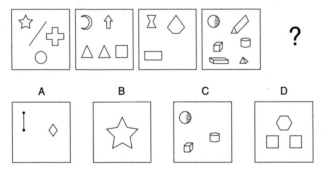

Answer: [   ]

Q3.

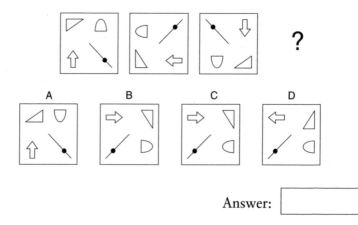

Answer:

Q4.

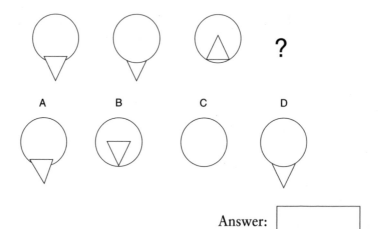

Answer:

Q5.

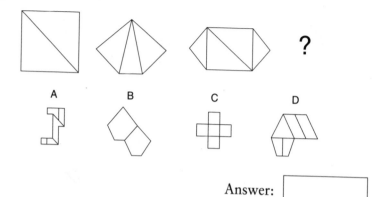

A   B   C   D

Answer: [   ]

End of test

Mini-test 4

Calculate the missing code.

Q1.

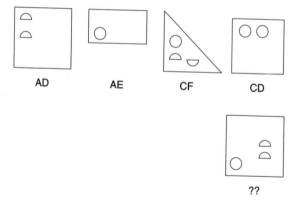

AD   AE   CF   CD

??

Suggested answers:

AE   CE   CD   AD

Answer: [   ]

Q2.

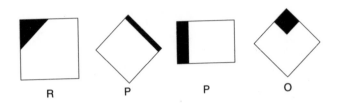

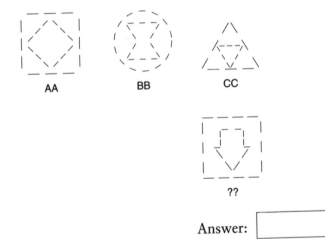

?

Answer: [   ]

Q3.

AA   BB   CC

??

Answer: [   ]

Q4.

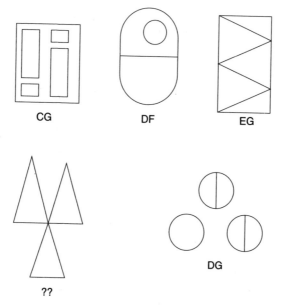

CG   DF   EG

??   DG

Answer: [   ]

Q5.

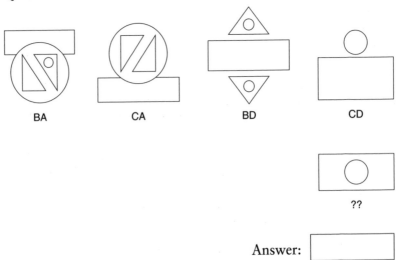

BA   CA   BD   CD

??

Answer:

End of test

Input-type diagrammatic reasoning tests

If you have been looking for practice for this sort of test then look no further. If you are applying for a position with a bank or professional service firm, or for a host of positions in management, scientific disciplines or engineering, then you may well face an input-type diagrammatic reasoning test.

These tests involve rules that must be applied to a sequence of either shapes or letters. They may involve symbols that change either figures or objects. For example, a symbol may signify that triangles must be replaced with squares. Alternatively, they may involve shapes that apply rules to a sequence of letters. For example, one shape will reverse the letters and another may signify that a letter must be dropped or added. These tests require you to visualize quickly how the sequence will change after a series of transformations.

Take the word 'quickly' seriously. Many candidates complain that there is insufficient time to attempt all the questions in this style of test. In many input-type diagrammatic reasoning tests the highest-scoring candidates are those who can maintain their accuracy while working quickly enough to attempt more questions than most other candidates. With practice you will be able to do this. There are 100 practice questions for this sort of test in this chapter.

There are four styles of question in this chapter. Review all of them irrespective of the sort of question you will face, because the benefit of this practice is transferable. You will find 10 examples of each type. Then you will find 12 mini-tests, each consisting of a new set of rules and five questions. Use the mini-tests to develop the all-important speed and accuracy that are essential if you want to achieve a high score in a real input-type diagrammatic reasoning test. In this type of test, practice really can make a difference to your score.

Type 1

Rules Q1–10:

AB Delete the last character
BC Replace the third character with the next in the alphabet
CD Insert the letter P between the third and fourth characters
DE Exchange the first and last characters
EF Replace the second character with the previous letter in the alphabet
FG Replace the fifth character with the next in the alphabet
GH Reverse the whole sequence of letters
HI Delete the third character

Q1.
MOZLUCK → AB + FG + CD →

(A) MOZPLVK
(B) MOZLVC
(C) MOZPLVCK
(D) MOZPLVC

Answer: [   ]

Q2.

CNPTTBM → HI + EF + DE →

(A) MMTTBC
(B) MMTTBM
(C) MNTTBC
(D) CMTTBC

Answer:

Q3.

GUAGEDR → BC + GH + FG →

(A) GUBGEDR
(B) DDGECUG
(C) RDEGCUG
(D) RDGEBUG

Answer:

Q4.

PBSATTS → HI + CD + FG →

(A) PBSPATTS
(B) PBAPUTS
(C) PBPATTS
(D) PBSAPTT

Answer:

Q5.

NOITIDE → AB + FG + GH →

(A) DITTON
(B) DITION
(C) DJTION
(D) EDITION

Answer:

Rules Q1–10:

AB Delete the last character
BC Replace the third character with the next in the alphabet
CD Insert the letter P between the third and fourth characters
DE Exchange the first and last characters
EF Replace the second character with the previous letter in the alphabet
FG Replace the fifth character with the next in the alphabet
GH Reverse the whole sequence of letters
HI Delete the third character

Q6.

GNISSAP → HI + GH + BC + FG →   (A) PATSOG
(B) PASSNG
(C) PANTGO
(D) PASSGNI

Answer: [   ]

Q7.

EQGTHST → DE + CD + BC + AB → (A) TQHPTHS
(B) EQHPTHS
(C) TQHPTHSE
(D) TQGPTHS

Answer: [   ]

Q8.

ANIHCS → GH + EF + CD + AB →   (A) AMIPHC
(B) SBHPIN
(C) SDHPINA
(D) CHINAS

Answer: [   ]

Q9.

TTOHSP → BC + FG + DE + HI →   (A) TTHTP
(B) PTHTP
(C) PTPHTT
(D) PTHTT

Answer:

Q10.

RCCUMJA → GH + CD + EF + GH →   (A) AIMUPCCA
(B) RICUPMMA
(C) RCCUPMIA
(D) RICUMJA

Answer:

Type 2

> *Rules Q11–20:*
>
> ¿   Remove all shading
> @   Switch the top and middle shapes
> Σ   Add a vertical line to the shape at the bottom of the series
> ♪   Switch the top and bottom shapes
> Ω   Replace the top shape with ▲
> ♱   Shade the second shape
> £   Replace the middle shape with ■
> ®   Switch the fourth and last shapes

Q11.

△
□
●   → ¿ + ♪ + ® →
⇩
⬠

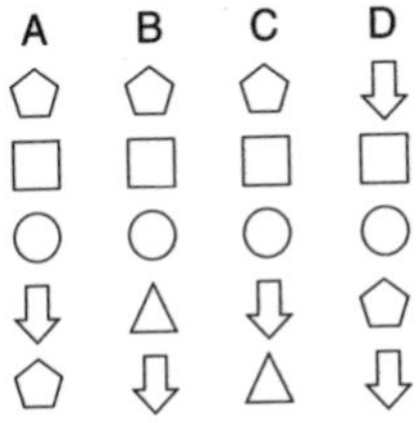

A	B	C	D
⬠	⬠	⬠	⇩
□	□	□	□
○	○	○	○
⇩	△	⇩	⬠
⬠	⇩	△	⇩

Answer: _____

Q12.

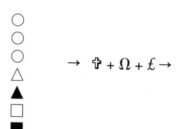

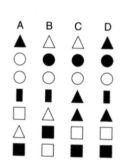

Answer: [   ]

Q13.

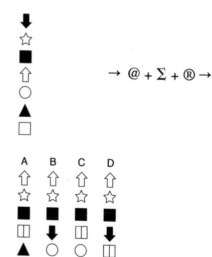

Answer: [   ]

Rules Q11–20:

¿   Remove all shading
@   Switch the top and middle shapes
Σ   Add a vertical line to the shape at the bottom of the series
♪   Switch the top and bottom shapes
Ω   Replace the top shape with ▲
♱   Shade the second shape
£   Replace the middle shape with ■
®   Switch the fourth and last shapes

Q14.

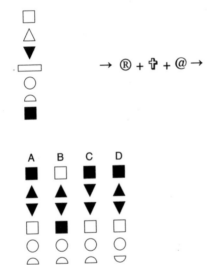

→ ® + ♱ + @ →

Answer:

Q15.

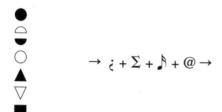

A	B	C	D

Answer:

Q16.

Answer:

Rules Q11–20:

¿ Remove all shading
@ Switch the top and middle shapes
Σ Add a vertical line to the shape at the bottom of the series
♪ Switch the top and bottom shapes
Ω Replace the top shape with ▲
✝ Shade the second shape
£ Replace the middle shape with ■
® Switch the fourth and last shapes

Q17.

→ ® + ✝ + Ω + ¿ →

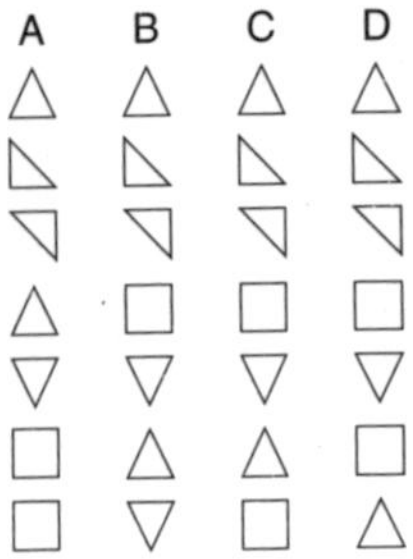

A	B	C	D
△	△	△	△
◁	◁	◁	◁
◥	◥	◥	◥
△	□	□	□
▽	▽	▽	▽
□	△	△	□
□	▽	□	△

Answer:

Q18.

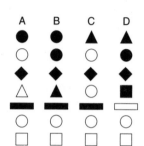

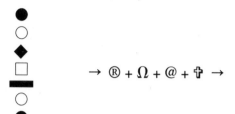

Answer:

Q19.

→ £ + ¿ + ® + ♪ →

Answer:

Rules Q11–20:

¿   Remove all shading
@   Switch the top and middle shapes
Σ   Add a vertical line to the shape at the bottom of the series
♪   Switch the top and bottom shapes
Ω   Replace the top shape with ▲
✇   Shade the second shape
£   Replace the middle shape with ■
®   Switch the fourth and last shapes

Q20.

$\rightarrow$ @ + ♪ + Ω + ® $\rightarrow$

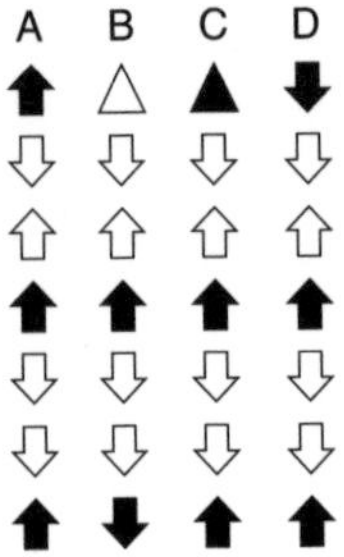

	A	B	C	D
	⬆	△	▲	⬇
	⇩	⇩	⇩	⇩
	⇧	⇧	⇧	⇧
	⬆	⬆	⬆	⬆
	⇩	⇩	⇩	⇩
	⇩	⇩	⇩	⇩
	⬆	⬇	⬆	⬆

Answer: [   ]

Type 3

Rules Q21–30:

☐	Reverse the whole sequence
△	Drop all Ts
○	Add TE to the end of the sequence
⬇	Exchange the first two and last two characters
☆	Add an A between the fourth and fifth characters
☐ △	Swap the first and second characters
○ ⬇	Drop the first A
○ ☐	Replace Es with Is
△ ○	Drop the second and fourth characters

Q21.

EYLLOHA → ☐ + ☐ △ + △ ○ →

A   HOLLY
B   HOLYE
C   HALLY
D   HAOLLYE   Answer: ⬚

Q22.

STNEMIN → ○ + ⬇ + ☆ →

A   TENEMINST
B   STNEMINTE
C   TENEAIMNST
D   TENEAMINST   Answer: ⬚

Rules Q21–30:

☐   Reverse the whole sequence

△   Drop all Ts

○   Add TE to the end of the sequence

⇩   Exchange the first two and last two characters

☆   Add an A between the fourth and fifth characters

☐ △   Swap the first and second characters

○ ⇩   Drop the first A

○ ☐   Replace Es with Is

△ ○   Drop the second and fourth characters

Q23.
FFOREST   → △ + ○ ☐ + ☐ →

A   TSEROFF
B   TSIOREST
C   SIROFF
D   SEROFF   Answer: [   ]

Q24.
CUCKOO   → ⇩ + ☆ + △ ○ →

A   OCACU
B   CUCKO
C   OOCAK
D   OCKCA   Answer: [   ]

Q25.

ENTHUSE   → ◯ ☐ + ☐ △ + ☐ →

A   ISUHTNI
B   NSUHTII
C   ISUHTIN
D   ISUTIHN   Answer: [   ]

Q26.

CAESAR   → ◯ ☐ + ◯ ⬇ + ☆ + ◯ ⬇ →

A   CISAR
B   CASIR
C   CISAAR
D   CISIR   Answer: [   ]

Q27.

AEOLIAN   → ◯ ⬇ + ◯ + ☆ + △ →

A   EOLOAANTE
B   EOLIANNE
C   EOLIANE
D   EOLIAANE   Answer: [   ]

Q28.

SENIOR   → ⬇ + ◯ + ◯ ☐ + ☐ →

A   ITISINOR
B   ITISINRO
C   ITESENRO
D   ITESINOR   Answer: [   ]

Rules Q21–30:

☐	Reverse the whole sequence
△	Drop all Ts
○	Add TE to the end of the sequence
⇩	Exchange the first two and last two characters
☆	Add an A between the fourth and fifth characters
☐ △	Swap the first and second characters
○ ⇩	Drop the first A
○ ☐	Replace Es with Is
△ ○	Drop the second and fourth characters

Q29.

ROIRRAW   → ☐ + ☐ △ + △ ○ + ☆ →

A   AWRIOR
B   ARIAOR
C   ARIOAR
D   ARRIOR

Answer: ☐

Q30.

TSERETNI   → △ + ○ ☐ + ○ + △ ○ →

A   SRNITE
B   SIRITNITE
C   SRINTIE
D   SIRTNTIE

Answer: ☐

Type 4

Rules Q31–40:

■   Cancel all shading

○   Shade the second and last shapes

●   Exchange the second and fourth shapes

□   Reverse the sequence of shapes

⬇   Change all circles to shaded squares

⇩   Replace all shaded shapes with unshaded triangles (with the apex at the top)

▲   Replace the first shape with a shaded triangle with its apex pointing downwards

△   Change the middle shape to an unshaded circle

Q31.

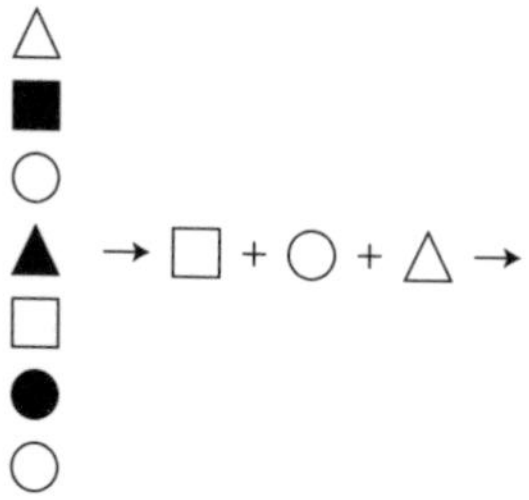

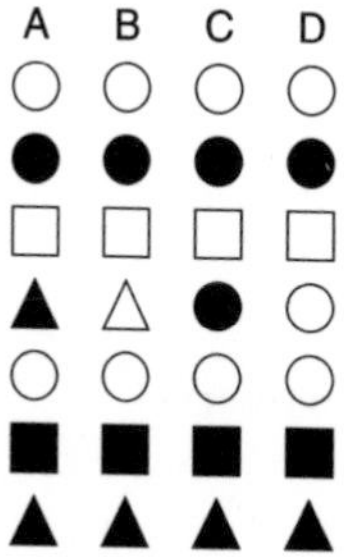

△
■
○
▲   → □ + ○ + △ →
□
●
○

A	B	C	D
○	○	○	○
●	●	●	●
□	□	□	□
▲	△	●	○
○	○	○	○
■	■	■	■
▲	▲	▲	▲

Answer: [   ]

Rules Q31–40:

■	Cancel all shading
○	Shade the second and last shapes
●	Exchange the second and fourth shapes
□	Reverse the sequence of shapes
⬇	Change all circles to shaded squares
⇩	Replace all shaded shapes with unshaded triangles (with the apex at the top)
▲	Replace the first shape with a shaded triangle with its apex pointing downwards
△	Change the middle shape to an unshaded circle

Q32.

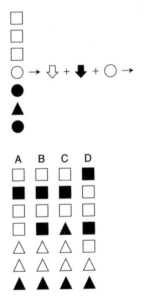

Answer:

Q33.

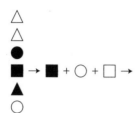

A	B	C	D
△	□	■	△
△	■	○	▲
○	○	△	○
□	△	□	□
△	□	○	△
○	○	▲	○
□	△	△	■
	▲		

Answer:

Q34.

▲
○
○
▲ → △ + ▲ + ⬇ →
▲
□
□

A	B	C	D
▼	▼	▽	▼
■	■	■	■
■	■	■	□
■	□	□	■
▲	▲	△	▽
□	□	■	■
□	□	■	□

Answer:

Rules Q31–40:

■	Cancel all shading
○	Shade the second and last shapes
●	Exchange the second and fourth shapes
□	Reverse the sequence of shapes
⬇	Change all circles to shaded squares
⇩	Replace all shaded shapes with unshaded triangles (with the apex at the top)
▲	Replace the first shape with a shaded triangle with its apex pointing downwards
△	Change the middle shape to an unshaded circle

Q35.

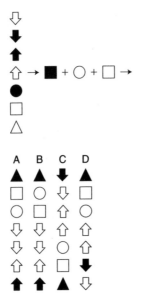

Answer: [   ]

Q36.

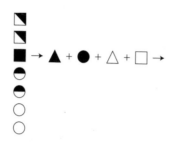

A	B	C	D
○	○	▽	○
○	○	◒	◒
◒	◒	■	○
○	○	○	●
■	■	◒	□
◒	◒	○	◒
▼	▽	○	▽

Answer:

Q37.

A	B	C	D
△	△	△	△
△	△	△	▲
△	△	△	△
△	▼	▲	△
□	□	□	□
△	▽	△	△
△	▲	▲	▲

Answer:

Rules Q31–40:

■	Cancel all shading
○	Shade the second and last shapes
●	Exchange the second and fourth shapes
□	Reverse the sequence of shapes
⬇	Change all circles to shaded squares
⇩	Replace all shaded shapes with unshaded triangles (with the apex at the top)
▲	Replace the first shape with a shaded triangle with its apex pointing downwards
△	Change the middle shape to an unshaded circle

Q38.

Answer:

Q39.

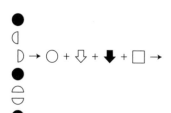

Answer: [   ]

Q40.

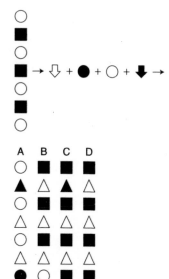

Answer: [   ]

Twelve mini-tests

Each test contains a set of rules and five input-type diagrammatic reasoning questions. The first questions are of average difficulty; then they become progressively harder. This is exactly what would happen in a real input-type diagrammatic reasoning test.

If you will be facing a test with one of the big banks or a professional services company, then give yourself four minutes to complete each mini-test. Otherwise allow yourself five minutes. Answers and explanations to these questions are found in Chapter 5.

Watch out for Mini-tests 8 and 11, because they involve a slightly different task to the ones you have practised so far. You will find two rows of letters or shapes, and the rules require you to switch between the two rows.

Insert your chosen answer in the answer box, and when you have checked your choice move quickly on to the next question.

Do not turn over the page until you are ready to begin.

Mini-test 1

Rules:

KL   Switch the second and fifth characters
MN   Replace the last character with the letter X
NO   Insert the letters SA between the sixth and seventh characters
PQ   Exchange the middle and last characters
RS   Switch the first and second characters
TU   Replace the first letter with the letter B
VW   Reverse the whole sequence of letters
XY   Replace the middle character with the letter C

Q1.

UVEFGKL → MN + RS + VW →

(A) XKGFEUV
(B) VUEFGKX
(C) XKGFEUX
(D) XFGKEUV

Answer: [   ]

Q2.

TENNINE → VW + PQ + NO →

(A) TENNESAT
(B) ENITNSEAN
(C) ENININSAT
(D) ENITNESAN

Answer: [   ]

Q3.

ZIALATER → KL + RS + TU →

(A) AZALITER
(B) BZAITER
(C) BZALITER
(D) BZACTIER

Answer: [   ]

Q4.

FIREDRI → KL + NO + VW + RS →   (A) ASIRIERDI
(B) AISRIERDF
(C) TASRIERDF
(D) FASIRERDI

Answer:

Q5.

DIAMOND → XY + TU + PQ + MN →   (A) CAIBONX
(B) BIADONX
(C) CIABONX
(D) CIAOBNX

Answer:

End of test

Mini-test 2

> *Rules:*
>
> AA   Replace the third letter with the number 3
> CC   Replace the last letter with the previous one in the alphabet
> GG   Delete the third item in the sequence
> II   Replace the fifth letter with the number 7
> KK   Replace the first number with the letter Z
> MM   Replace the first letter with the number 9
> OO   Replace the fourth item with the letters WR

Q1.

BA2W3KEV → AA + II + MM →

(A) 9A3WKE7
(B) 9BA23KE7
(C) 9A233KE7
(D) 9A332KE7

Answer: [ ]

Q2.

WNPK999R → GG + KK + OO →

(A) WNKWR999R
(B) WNKWR99R
(C) 9NKWR99R
(D) ZNKRW99R

Answer: [ ]

Q3.

ARL4599ABC → CC + AA + II + OO →

(A) AR3WR999AB7
(B) RA3WR999AB7
(C) RA3WR559AB7
(D) AR3WR599AB7

Answer: [ ]

Q4.

A2N5N7DE → II + MM + GG + CC →   (A) 925N7C7
                                   (B) 925N7E7
                                   (C) 925N7D7
                                   (D) 925M7D7

Answer: [   ]

Q5.

35HIRB83 → AA + GG + OO + KK →   (A) Z5WR3B83
                                  (B) 351WRB83
                                  (C) Z5HWRB83
                                  (D) Z35WRB83

Answer: [   ]

End of test

Mini-test 3

Rules:

ZY Change the third letter to lower case
XW Insert the letters Nr between the first and second items
VU Exchange the second and sixth items in the sequence
TS Change the first letter to lower case
RQ Replace the second lower-case letter with the next in the alphabet
PO Exchange the first and last items in the sequence
NM Replace the second number with an upper-case P
LK Replace the fourth lower-case letter with the next in the alphabet

Q1.
2007GMATgat → ZY + TS + NM →

(A) 2P07GMATgat
(B) 2P07gMaTgat
(C) 2P07gmatgat
(D) 2p07GMatgat

Answer: ☐

Q2.
UKCAT2008bmat → LK + NM + RQ →

(A) UKCAT2p08bNau
(B) UKCAT2P08bnaU
(C) UKCAT2P08bnau
(D) UKCAT2P07bnua

Answer: ☐

Q3.

inter555MAR → XW + PO + VU →

(A) RrteN555MAi
(B) RrrteN55MMAi
(C) RrteN555Mai
(D) RerntNr555MAi

Answer: _____

Q4.

RaTio16naLe → ZY + VU + TS + PO →

(A) e1tioa6naLr
(B) r1tioa6naLe
(C) R1tioa6naLe
(D) eatio16naLe

Answer: _____

Q5.

UST65char → LK + NM + PO + RQ →

(A) sST6pchaU
(B) UST6Pchas
(C) sST6PdhaU
(D) sST6PchaU

Answer: _____

End of test

Mini-test 4

Rules:

§   Replace the first shape with a ▲
♪   Switch the positions of the second and last shapes
¶   Replace every ▲ with a ▮
‰ Change the fourth shape to an unshaded circle
¤   Move the third shape to the bottom of the sequence
%   Shade all circles
<   Replace all shaded squares with unshaded diamonds
>   Move the sixth shape to the top of the sequence

Q1.

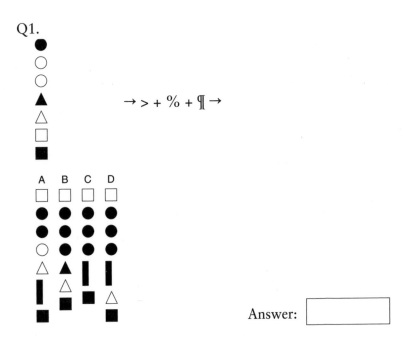

→ > + % + ¶ →

Answer:

Q2.

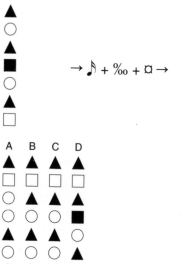

Answer: [   ]

Q3.

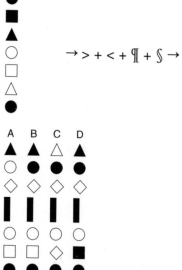

Answer: [   ]

Rules:

§	Replace the first shape with a ▲
♪	Switch the positions of the second and last shapes
¶	Replace every ▲ with a ▮
‰	Change the fourth shape to an unshaded circle
¤	Move the third shape to the bottom of the sequence
%	Shade all circles
<	Replace all shaded squares with unshaded diamonds
>	Move the sixth shape to the top of the sequence

Q4.

□
▲
□
□
▲
●
●

→ ♪ + ‰ + % + > →

	A	B	C	D
	▲	▲	●	●
	□	□	□	□
	●	○	●	●
	□	■	□	□
	●	○	○	●
	△	▲	▲	▲
	●	○	▲	▲

Answer: [   ]

Q5.

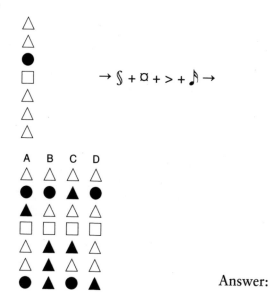

Answer: [   ]

End of test

Mini-test 5

> *Rules:*
>
> (Move the top shape to the bottom of the sequence
> @   Add an unshaded square after the first shaded shape
>)   Move the second-from-last shape to the middle of the sequence
> #   Change the bottom shape into a shaded triangle
> Σ   Shade the last unshaded shape
> ∞   Replace the third shape with a shaded square
> ≤   Move the second shape and place it between the fifth and sixth shapes
> δ   Remove the third shape from the sequence

Q1.

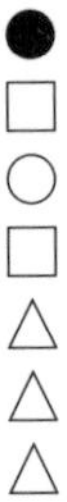

$\rightarrow$ (+ # + Σ →

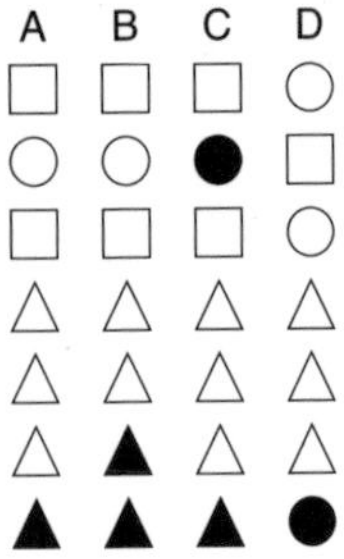

A   B   C   D

Answer:

Q2.

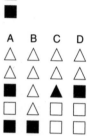 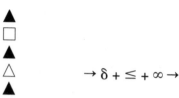

A	B	C	D
△	△	△	△
△	△	△	△
■	△	▲	■
□	△	□	□
■	■	□	□
□	■	□	■

Answer: [   ]

Q3.

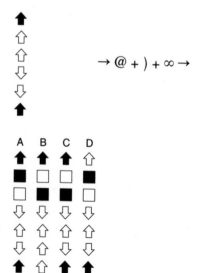

Answer: [   ]

Rules:

(Move the top shape to the bottom of the sequence
@   Add an unshaded square after the first shaded shape
)   Move the second-from-last shape to the middle of the sequence
Change the bottom shape into a shaded triangle
Σ   Shade the last unshaded shape
∞   Replace the third shape with a shaded square
≤   Move the second shape and place it between the fifth and sixth
       shapes
δ   Remove the third shape from the sequence

Q4.

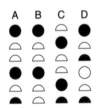

$\rightarrow \delta + \leq + (+ \Sigma \rightarrow$

   A   B   C   D

Answer: [　　　　　　]

Q5.

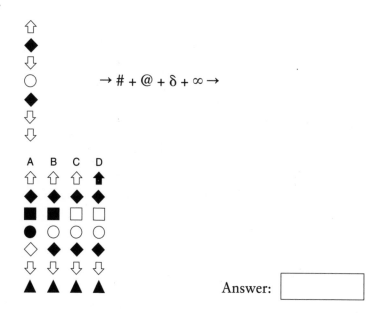

Answer: [   ]

End of test

Mini-test 6

> *Rules:*
>
> ↔   Reverse the order of the shapes
> ↕   Replace all unshaded circles with shaded squares
> ≠   Reverse all shading (ie shade unshaded shapes and remove the shading from shaded shapes)
> «   Replace all unshaded triangles with shaded triangles
> »   Insert an unshaded square between the third and fourth shapes
> ⅏   Remove the sixth item from the sequence
> ⊗   Switch the second and fourth shapes
> ∩   Shade the third and fifth shapes if they are not already shaded

Q1.

→ ≠ + ⅏ + ⊗ →

Answer:

Q2.

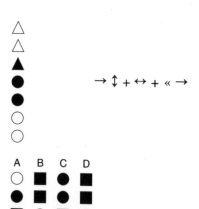

Answer:

Q3.

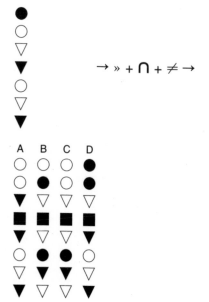

Answer:

Rules:

↔	Reverse the order of the shapes
↕	Replace all unshaded circles with shaded squares
≠	Reverse all shading (ie shade unshaded shapes and remove the shading from shaded shapes)
«	Replace all unshaded triangles with shaded triangles
»	Insert an unshaded square between the third and fourth shapes
✄	Remove the sixth item from the sequence
⊗	Switch the second and fourth shapes
∩	Shade the third and fifth shapes if they are not already shaded

Q4.

$$\rightarrow \updownarrow + ✄ + \neq + \leftrightarrow \rightarrow$$

A B C D

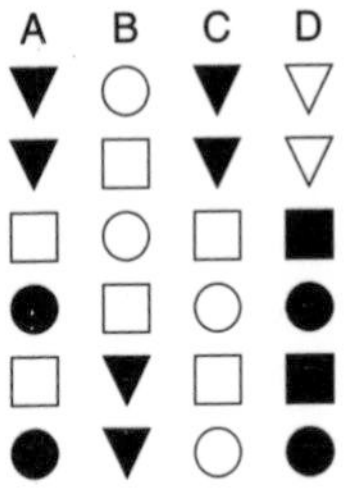

Answer:

Q5.

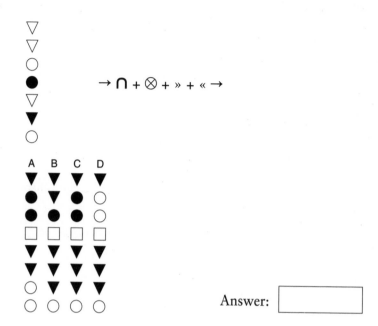

Answer: ☐

End of test

Mini-test 7

Rules:

☐ ☐	Switch the second and last characters in the series
○ ○	Insert the letter W after the first character
△ △	Delete the fifth character
☐ ○	Switch the fourth and fifth characters
☐ △	Delete the second character
○ ☐	Insert the letter B between the third and fourth characters
○ △	Delete the sixth character
△ ☐	Switch the last two characters in the sequence
△ ○	Insert the letter M after the fourth character

Q1.

MNEMONIC   → △ ○ + ○ △ + ☐ ○ →

A   MNEMNMIC
B   MNEMMOIC
C   MNEMMNIC
D   MNMEMNIC

Answer: ☐

Q2.

DINGDONG   → ☐ ☐ + ○ ○ + △ △ →

A   DWGNDONI
B   GWINDGOND
C   GWIGDOND
D   GINGDONG

Answer: ☐

Q3.

QUADRANT   → △ △ + □ ○ + ○ □ →

A   QUAADBNT
B   QUAABDNT
C   QUABRADNT
D   QUABADNT

Answer: [   ]

Q4.

COSTUME   → △ □ + □ △ + △ ○ →

A   CSTMUEM
B   CSTUMEM
C   CSTUEM
D   CSUTMUEM

Answer: [   ]

Q5.

INVISIBLE   → △ □ + □ □ + △ △ + □ ○ →

A   ILIVIBEN
B   ILVIIBEN
C   ILVIBIEN
D   ILISIBEN

Answer: [   ]

End of test

Mini-test 8

Rules:

△▽ Exchange the fourth character between the two sequences

◁▷ Reverse the top sequence

▽△ Insert the letter N after the second character in the lower sequence

▽▽ Reverse the lower sequence

△△ Exchange the fifth character between the two sequences

◁◁ Exchange the second and fourth characters in the top sequence

▷▷ Insert the letter L after the fifth character in the top sequence

▷◁ Exchange the first and last characters in the lower sequence

Q1.

PLACON
OPTIC
→ △▽ + ▽△ + ◁◁ →

A PILAON
   OPTCO
B PLAION
   CPTCO
C PIALON
   OPNTCC
D PLAION
   CPTCO

Answer: [＿＿＿＿＿]

Q2.

DENSTY
GANIUM   → ▷▷ + △/▽ + ▷◁ →

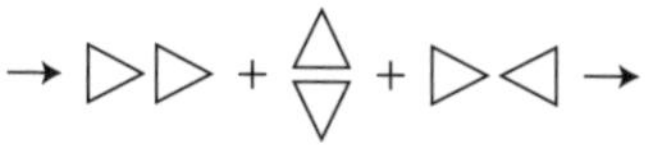

A   DENITLY
    MANSUG
B   DENSTLY
    MUSNAG
C   DENSTLY
    MANSUG
D   DENITLY
    MUSNAG

Answer: [   ]

Q3.

CYCLIZE
MOLLUSC   → △/△ + ▽/▽ + △/▽ →

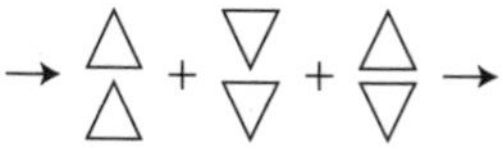

A   CYCLUZE
    CSILLOM
B   CYILUZE
    CSCLLOM
C   CYCLLOM
    CYILUZE
D   CYCLUZE
    MOLLUSC

Answer: [   ]

Rules:

△▽   Exchange the fourth character between the two sequences

◁▷   Reverse the top sequence

▽△   Insert the letter N after the second character in the lower sequence

▽▽   Reverse the lower sequence

△△   Exchange the fifth character between the two sequences

◁◁   Exchange the second and fourth characters in the top sequence

▷▷   Insert the letter L after the fifth character in the top sequence

▷◁   Exchange the first and last characters in the lower sequence

Q4.

ROTTEN   → ▽△ + ▷▷ + ▷◁ →
VESPER

A   ROTTENL
     RENSPEV
B   ROTTELN
     RENSPEV
C   ROTTLEN
     RESPNEV
D   ROTTELN
     RESNPEV

Answer: [   ]

Q5.

ENWRAP
REVISE

$\rightarrow \triangleq + \triangleleft\triangleleft + \triangledown \rightarrow$

A EIWNAP
ERSVER
B EINWAP
ERSVER
C EINWAP
ESRVER
D EIWNAP
ESRVER

Answer: [   ]

End of test

Mini-test 9

Rules:

☐   If the current version of the sequence contains the letter I then delete the first letter; otherwise delete the last letter

○   Add BP to the beginning of the sequence

◇   Swap the third and fifth characters in the sequence

▽   Insert the letter P between the second and third characters

△   Insert the letter Z between the sixth and seventh characters

⬠   Exchange the last two characters in the sequence

☆   Reverse the sequence

◠   Insert the letter H between the third and fourth characters

⧄   Swap the first and last characters in the sequence

⬡   If the current version of the sequence contains the letter E delete the third character; otherwise delete the fourth character

Q1.
UMBRELLA   → ⧄ + ☆ + ▽ →

A   ULLPERBMA
B   ULPLERBMA
C   ALLPERBMU
D   ALPLERBMU

Answer: ☐

Q2.
MUNICPAL   → ⬠ + △ + ◠ →

A   MUHHICZPLA
B   MUNHICPZLA
C   MUHNICPZLA
D   MUNHICZPLA

Answer: ☐

Q3.

HAMMOCK   → ◇ + ⬡ + ◯ + ☆ →

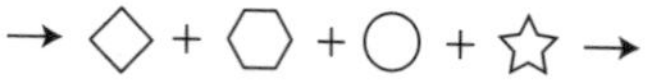

A   KMOMHABP
B   KMOMHAPB
C   KMOMAHBP
D   KCMOAHPB

Answer: _____

Q4.

DRIBBLE   → ▽ + △ + ⬠ + ☐ →

A   RPBIBZEL
B   DRPIBBZE
C   RPIBBZEL
D   RPIBBZLE

Answer: _____

Q5.

COLUMNIST   → ◇ + ⌒ + ☐ + ☆ →

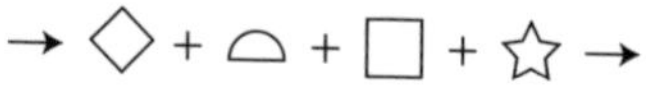

A   CTSINLUHM
B   TSINLUHMO
C   OMHULNIST
D   TISNLUHMO

Answer: _____

End of test

Mini-test 10

Rules:

☐   Reverse the sequence of shapes

◯   Only shade every second shape in the series (if any shapes are already shaded then unshade them)

△   Change all shaded circles to shaded squares

■   Change all shaded triangles to shaded circles

●   Exchange the first and last shaded shapes

▲   Shade all triangles

▽   Reverse all shading

▼   Remove the shading from all squares

Q1.

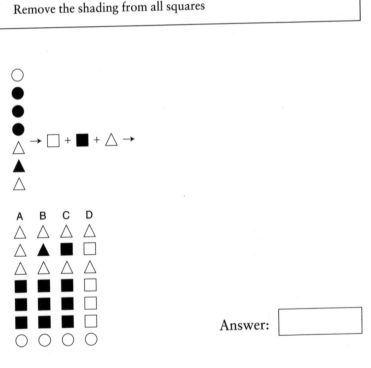

Answer: [   ]

Q2.

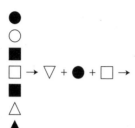

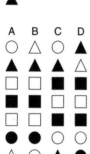

Answer: _____

Q3.

□
□
□
△ → ○ + ▼ + ■ →
△
△
○

A	B	C	D
□	□	□	□
□	□	□	□
■	□	□	□
□	□	●	▲
△	△	△	△
□	□	●	□
○	○	○	○

Answer: _____

Rules:

☐	Reverse the sequence of shapes
◯	Only shade every second shape in the series (if any shapes are already shaded then unshade them)
△	Change all shaded circles to shaded squares
◼	Change all shaded triangles to shaded circles
●	Exchange the first and last shaded shapes
▲	Shade all triangles
▽	Reverse all shading
▼	Remove the shading from all squares

Q4.

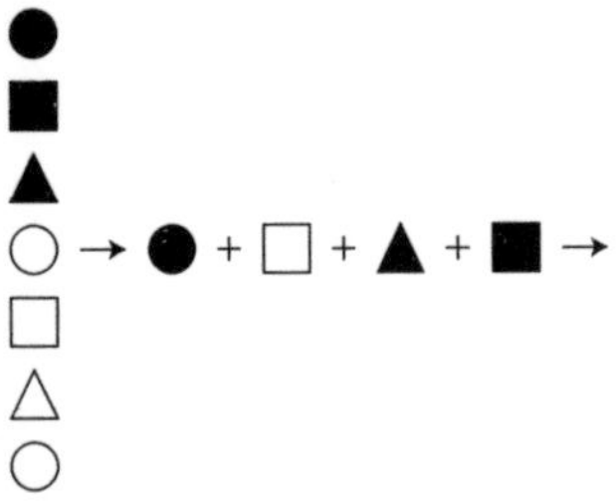

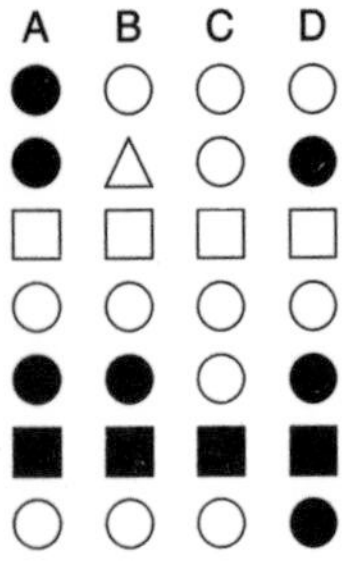

● ▪ ▲ ◯ □ △ ◯ → ● + □ + ▲ + ■ →

A	B	C	D
●	◯	◯	◯
●	△	◯	●
□	□	□	□
◯	◯	◯	◯
●	●	◯	●
■	■	■	■
◯	◯	◯	●

Answer: [＿＿＿＿]

Q5.

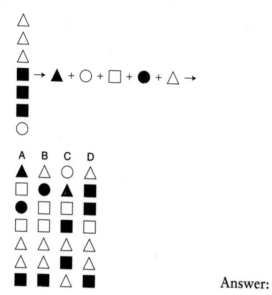

Answer: [   ]

End of test

Mini-test 11

Rules:

⬇ Exchange the first and last shapes between the top and bottom sequences

⬆ Reverse the shading in the top sequence

⬇ Exchange the middle shapes between the top and bottom sequences

⬆ Shade all squares and circles

☆ Exchange the second-from-last shapes between the top and bottom sequences

★ Reverse all shading

⬠ Exchange the third and fifth shapes between the top and bottom sequences

⬠ Reverse the shading in the bottom sequence

Q1.

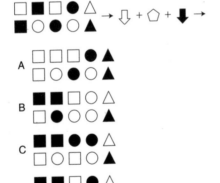

Answer: [   ]

Q2.

● ● ● ○ ○
□ ■ △ ▲ △ → ☆ + ★ + ⬇ →

A
○ ○ ○ △ ●
■ □ ▲ ● ▲

B
○ ○ ▲ △ ●
■ □ ○ ● ▲

C
● ○ ▲ △ ●
■ □ ○ ● ▲

D
○ ○ ▲ △ ●
■ □ ▲ ● ▲

Answer: [   ]

Q3.

▼ ▼ ▼ □ ■
○ ○ ▼ ▼ ○ → ⇧ + ⇩ + ☆ →

A
○ ▽ ▽ ▼ ○
▽ ○ ▼ ■ □

B
○ ▽ ▽ ▼ □
▽ ○ ▼ ■ ○

C
○ ▽ ▽ ▼ ○
▽ ○ ▼ ▼ □

D
○ ▽ ▽ ▼ □
▽ ○ ▼ ■ ○

Answer: [   ]

Rules:

⬇ (outline) Exchange the first and last shapes between the top and bottom sequences

⬆ (outline) Reverse the shading in the top sequence

⬇ (filled) Exchange the middle shapes between the top and bottom sequences

⬆ (filled) Shade all squares and circles

☆ (outline star) Exchange the second-from-last shapes between the top and bottom sequences

★ (filled star) Reverse all shading

⬠ (outline pentagon) Exchange the third and fifth shapes between the top and bottom sequences

⬟ (filled pentagon) Reverse the shading in the bottom sequence

Q4.

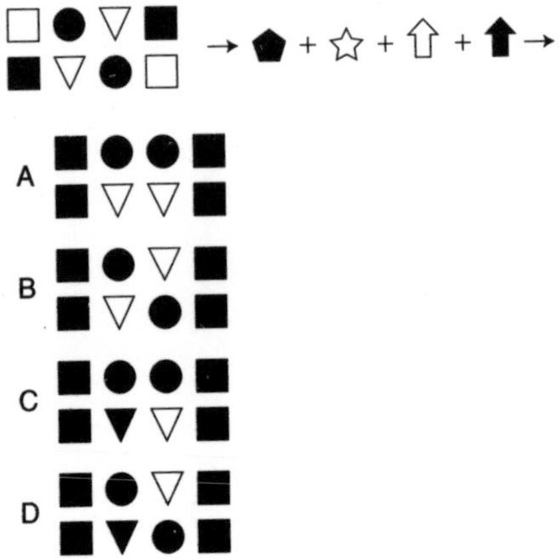

□ ● ▽ ■   → ⬟ + ☆ + ⬆ + ⬆ →
■ ▽ ● □

A ■ ● ● ■
   ■ ▽ ▽ ■

B ■ ● ▽ ■
   ■ ▽ ● ■

C ■ ● ● ■
   ■ ▼ ▽ ■

D ■ ● ▽ ■
   ■ ▼ ● ■

Answer: [   ]

Q5.

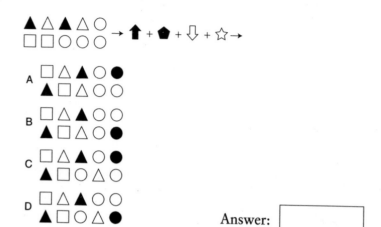

Answer: [   ]

End of test

Mini-test 12

Rules:

□ △	Exchange the first and third shapes
△ □	Change all triangles into shaded circles
□ ▲	Exchange the fourth and sixth shapes
△ ■	Reverse the shading of the first and fifth shapes
■ △	Reverse the shading
▲ □	Change all shaded circles to unshaded squares
□ □	Reverse the sequence of shapes
■ ■	Change all unshaded squares to unshaded triangles
△ △	Exchange the middle and last shapes
▲ ▲	Reverse the shading of the second and second-from-last shapes

Q1.

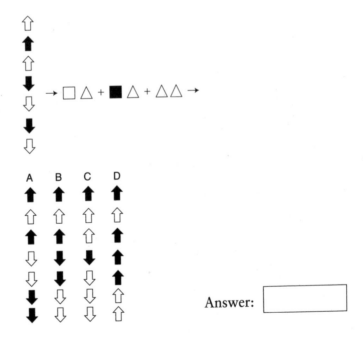

Answer: [　　　　]

Q2.

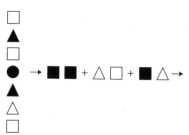

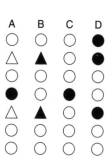

A	B	C	D
○	○	○	●
△	▲	○	●
○	○	○	○
●	○	●	○
△	▲	○	●
○	○	○	○
○	○	○	○

Answer: [   ]

Q3.

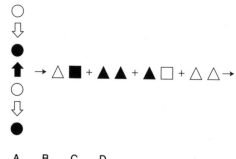

A	B	C	D
□	□	□	□
⬇	⬇	⇩	⬇
□	□	□	□
□	⬇	□	□
□	□	□	□
⬇	⬇	⇩	⬇
⬇	□	⇩	⬆

Answer: [   ]

Rules:

□ △	Exchange the first and third shapes
△ □	Change all triangles into shaded circles
□ ▲	Exchange the fourth and sixth shapes
△ ■	Reverse the shading of the first and fifth shapes
■ △	Reverse the shading
▲ □	Change all shaded circles to unshaded squares
□ □	Reverse the sequence of shapes
■ ■	Change all unshaded squares to unshaded triangles
△ △	Exchange the middle and last shapes
▲ ▲	Reverse the shading of the second and second-from-last shapes

Q4.

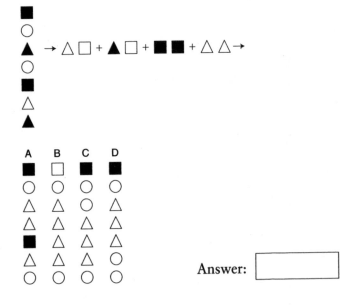

Answer: [   ]

Q5.

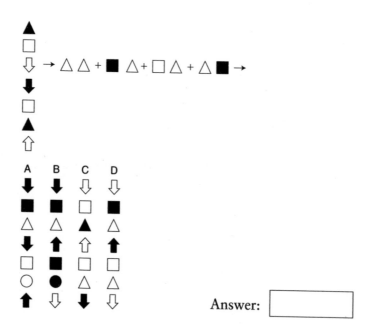

Answer: _____

End of test

Conceptual or spatial reasoning tests

Have you ever faced a test that involves two- and three-dimensional shapes and requires you to transform or manipulate them mentally? These are conceptual or spatial reasoning tests. You may, for example, be required to identify a shape's mirror image or its net (what it will look like if 'unfolded' and made flat). In other instances you are required to identify a shape correctly from a particular perspective or after it has been rotated. You are presented with a series of suggested answers from which to choose the correct transformation or manipulation. To make things deliberately more difficult, the suggested answers are often very similar or intentionally misleading. As with every test the questions start off relatively easy and become progressively more difficult. Towards the end of a test the questions, shapes and suggested answers are really quite complex. You often have to work against a tight time limit.

These tests are commonly used for the selection of candidates for positions in design, the technical crafts, engineering and science. For example, architects and mechanical engineers may well face these tests as a part of the recruitment process for a job or place on a training programme.

This chapter contains 100 practice questions that imitate the typical demands found in real tests of this sort. As in a real test the practice questions start easy and get progressively harder. Some of these practice questions are difficult! Use them to practise your time management. Do not spend too long on one question, and use informed guessing – rule out some of the suggested answers as wrong and, in the process, improve your chances of correctly guessing the answer.

This section begins with examples of the five typical sorts of question and then finishes with 10 mini-tests. Enjoy!

Type 1

These are probably the most common sort of spatial reasoning question, and they require you to identify what a three-dimensional shape becomes if it is 'unfolded' to a flat shape (what is called in geometry the 'net'). You must choose the correct net of the three-dimensional question shape from three or four suggested answers, but take care, because as already mentioned they are often very similar or intentionally misleading. Try the following 10 examples. You will find six net-type mini-tests later in the chapter.

Q1.

A

B

C

D

Answer:

Q2.

A

B

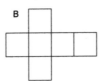

C

D

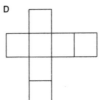

Answer:

Q3.

A
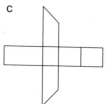

B

C
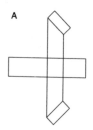

D

Answer:

Q4.

A
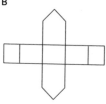

B
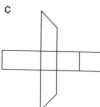

C
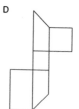

D

Answer:

Q5.

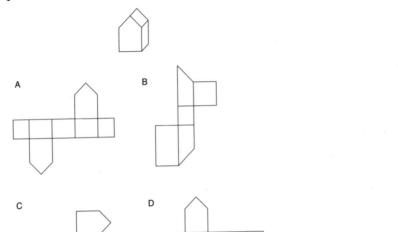

Answer: [   ]

Q6.

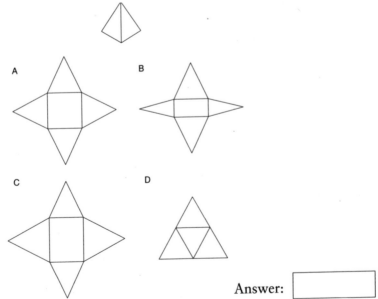

Answer: [   ]

Q7.

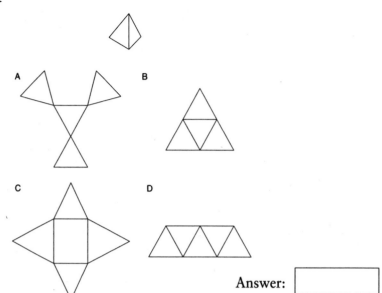

A   B

C   D

Answer:

Q8.

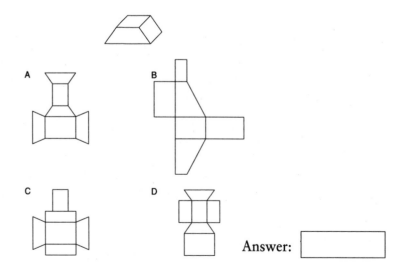

A   B

C   D

Answer:

Q9.

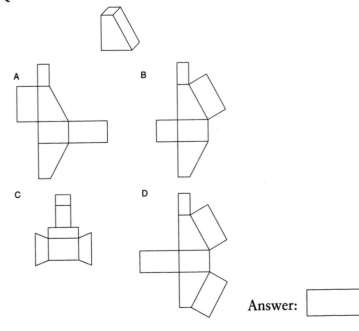

Answer: [   ]

Q10.

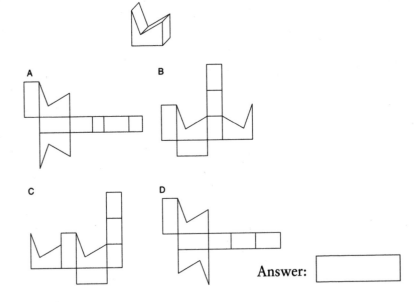

Answer: [   ]

Type 2

In these questions you must identify the plan of the three-dimensional question shape. A plan is the view of the shape looking exactly downwards. In other words you must identify the figure that correctly represents how the top of a geometric shape will look. This style of question is used in trainability tests for engineers, for example.

Q11.

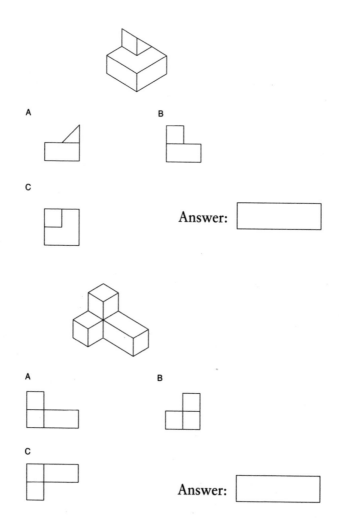

Q12.

Answer:

Answer:

Q13.

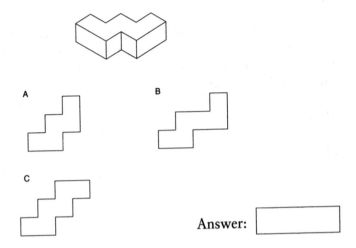

A

B

C

Answer:

Q14.

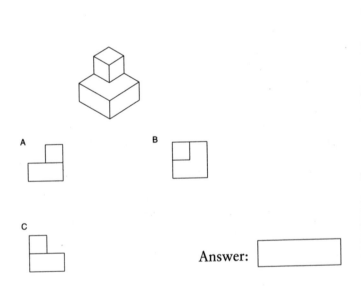

A

B

C

Answer:

Q15.

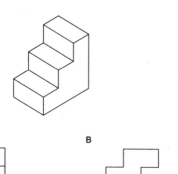

A

B

C

Answer:

Q16.

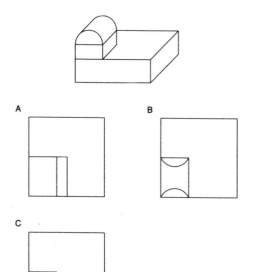

A

B

C

Answer:

Q17.

A

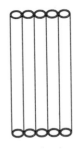

B

C

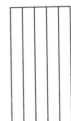

Answer: [   ]

Q18.

A

B

C

Answer: [   ]

Q19.

A

B

C

Answer: [ ]

Q20.

A

B

C

Answer: [ ]

Type 3

In this style of spatial reasoning question you must identify the mirror image of the shape. If the mirror image has also been rotated it is incorrect. Try the following 10 examples. You will also find two mini-tests on which to practise this style of question against a time limit.

Q21.

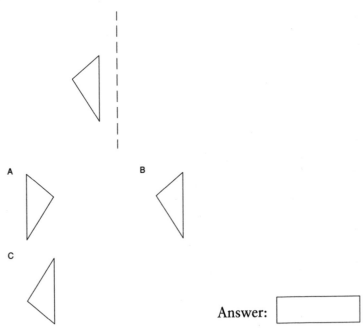

Answer: ☐

Q22.

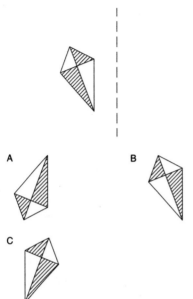

Answer: [   ]

Q23.

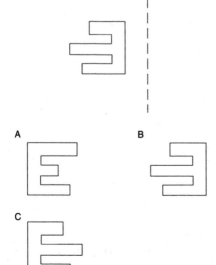

Answer: [   ]

Q24.

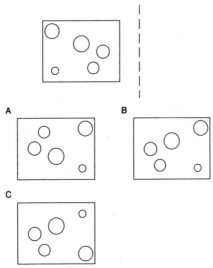

Answer: [   ]

Q25.

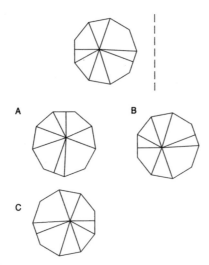

Answer: [   ]

Q26.

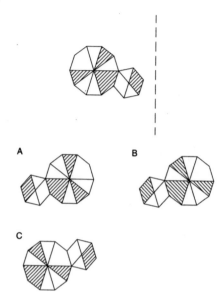

Answer: [   ]

Q27.

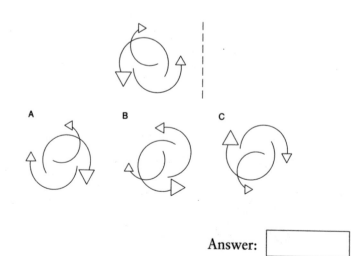

Answer: [   ]

Q28.

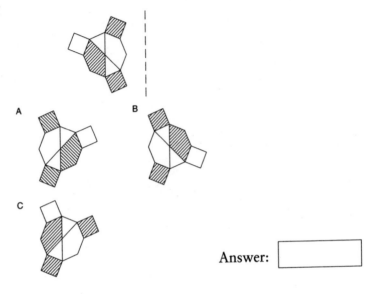

A   B

C

Answer: [   ]

Q29.

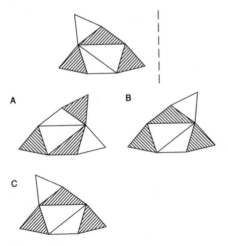

A   B

C

Answer: [   ]

Q30.

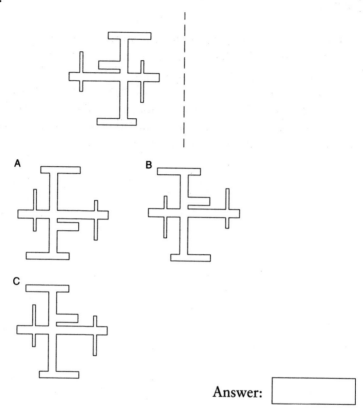

Answer:

Type 4

In this type of spatial question the question shape is rotated. Your task is to identify the shape that has been rotated but is otherwise identical to the question shape. The extent and direction of rotation vary from question to question, but only one suggested shape is the same as the question shape. All the others will have been rotated and/or changed in some other way as well. Try the following 10 examples. There are also two mini-tests.

Q31.

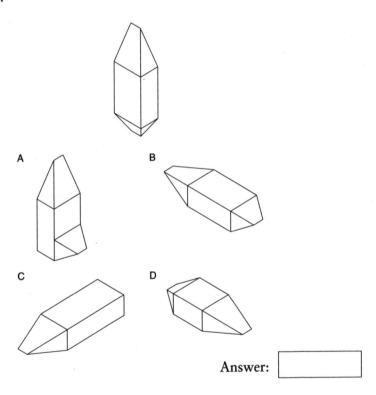

Answer:

Q32.

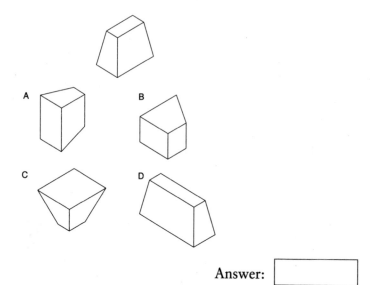

Answer: [   ]

Q33.

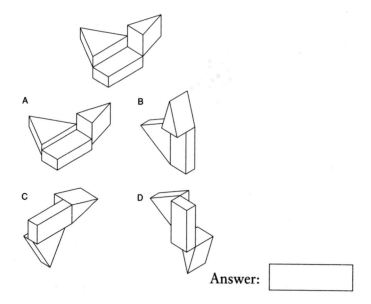

Answer: [   ]

Q34.

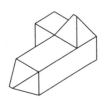

A 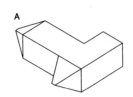   B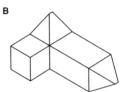

C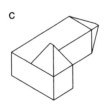

Answer:

Q35.

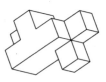

A 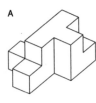   B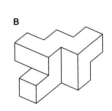

C

Answer:

Q36.

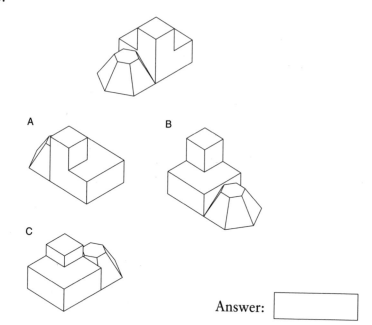

A

B

C

Answer:

Q37.

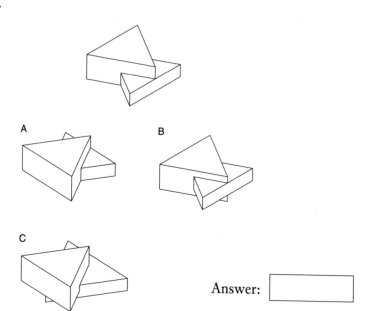

A

B

C

Answer:

Q38.

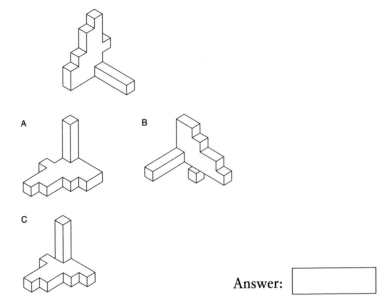

A   B

C

Answer: [   ]

Q39.

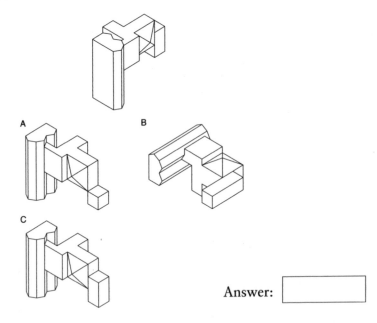

A   B

C

Answer: [   ]

Q40.

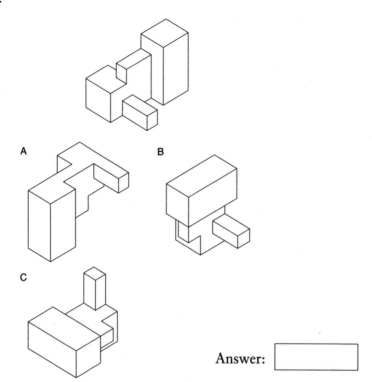

A

B

C

Answer:

Type 5

In this style of spatial question your task is to identify the new shape that could be constructed if the two example shapes were combined. No other change should be made to the two shapes other than combining them. Try the following 10 examples.

Q41.

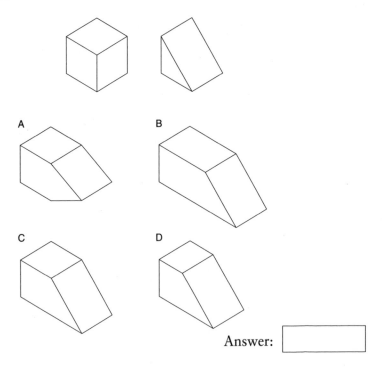

Answer:

Q42.

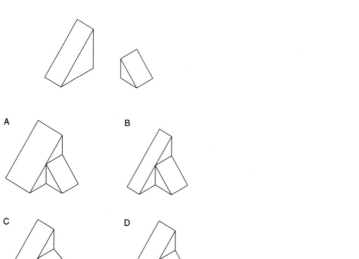

A   B

C   D   Answer:

Q43.

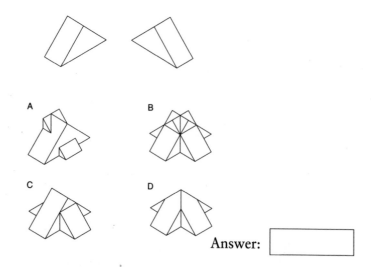

A   B

C   D   Answer:

Q44.

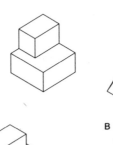

A

B

C

Answer: [   ]

Q45.

A

B

C

Answer: [   ]

Q46.

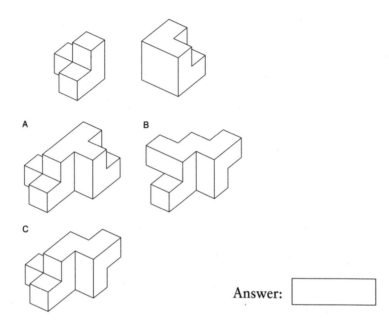

Answer: [   ]

Q47.

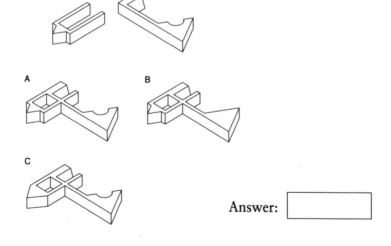

Answer: [   ]

Q48.

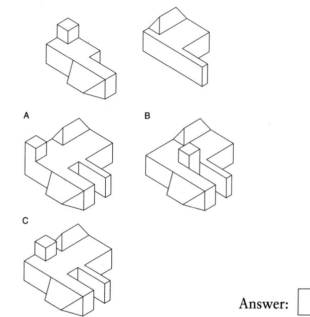

Answer: [   ]

Q49.

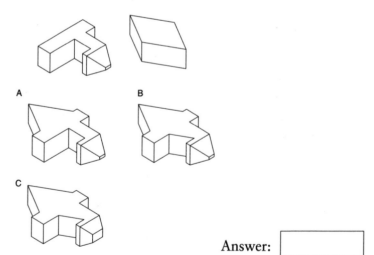

Answer: [   ]

Q50.

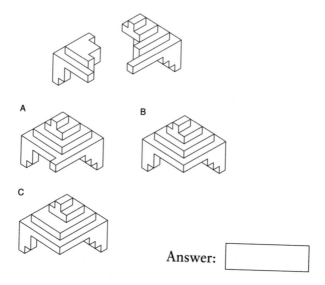

A

B

C

Answer:

Ten mini-tests

Each of the following practice tests contains five multiple-choice questions. The first is of average difficulty, and they become progressively harder. This is exactly what would happen in a real spatial reasoning test.

Set yourself the time limit of four minutes in which to complete each practice test. Answers and explanations are found in Chapter 5.

Insert your chosen answer in the answer box, and when you have checked your choice move on to the next question.

The first six mini-tests are concerned with nets. In Mini-tests 1–4 you are presented with a three-dimensional shape and must identify its net. Mini-tests 5 and 6 require you to undertake a related but different task. The question shape is a net, and you must identify the 3D shape that correctly relates to it.

Do not turn the page until you are ready to begin Mini-test 1.

Mini-test 1

Identify the 3D shape's net.

Q1.

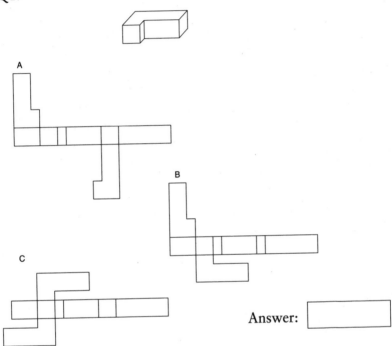

Answer:

Q2.

A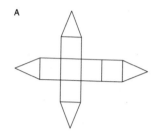

B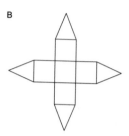

C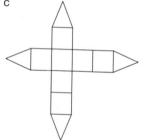

Answer:

Q3.

A

B

C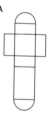

Answer:

Q4.

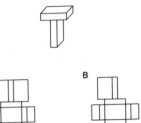

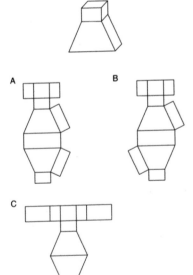

Answer: [   ]

Q5.

End of test

Mini-test 2

Identify the 3D shape's net.

Q1.

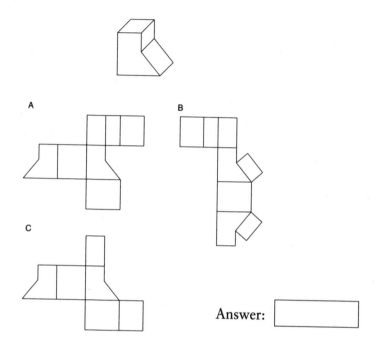

A

B

C

Answer:

Q2.

A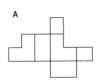

B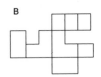

C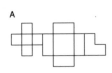

Answer: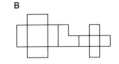

Q3.

A

B

C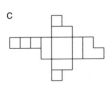

Answer:

Q4.

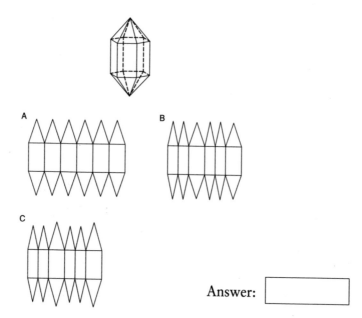

Answer: [   ]

Q5.

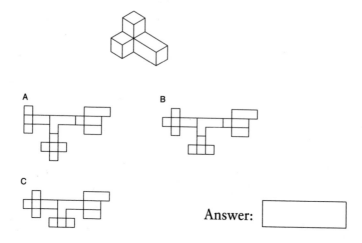

Answer: [   ]

End of test

Mini-test 3

Identify the 3D shape's net.

Q1.

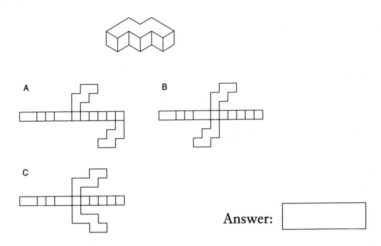

Answer: [   ]

Q2.

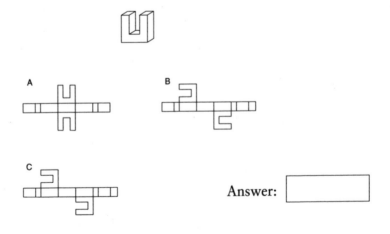

Answer: [   ]

Q3.

A 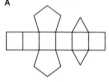   B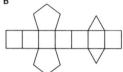

C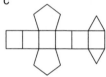

Answer: [   ]

Q4.

A 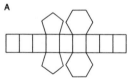   B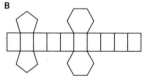

C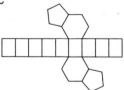

Answer: [   ]

Q5.

A

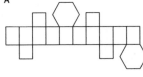

B

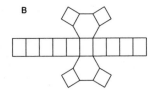

C

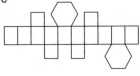

Answer: [   ]

End of test

Mini-test 4

Identify the 3D question shape's net.

Q1.

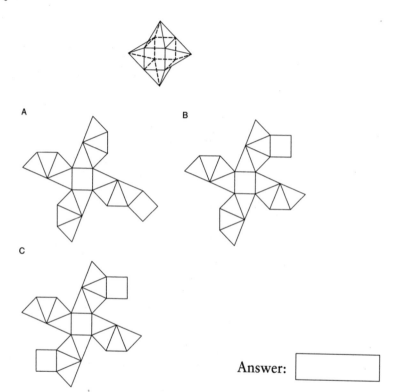

A

B

C

Answer:

Q2.

A

B

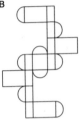

C

Answer:

Q3.

A

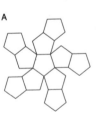

B

C

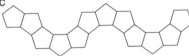

Answer:

Q4.

A

B

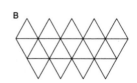

C

Answer: [   ]

Q5.

A

B

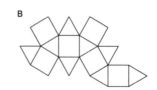

C

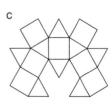

Answer: [   ]

End of test

Mini-test 5

Identify the 3D shape that correctly corresponds to the question net.

Q1.

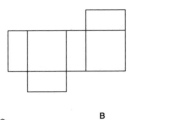

Answer: [   ]

Q2.

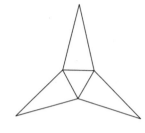

A

B

C

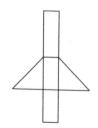

D

Answer: [   ]

Q3.

A

B

C

D

Answer: [   ]

Q4.

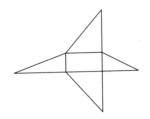

A   B

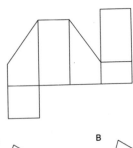

C

Answer:

Q5.

A   B

C

Answer:

End of test

Mini-test 6

Identify the 3D shape that correctly corresponds to the question net.

Q1.

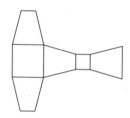

A

B

C

Answer: [   ]

Q2.

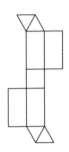

A

B

C

Answer:

Q3.

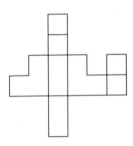

A

B

C

Answer:

Q4.

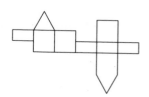

A   B

C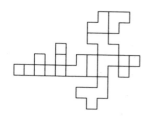

Answer:

Q5.

A   B

C

Answer:

End of test

Mini-test 7

Identify the mirror image of the question shape.

Q1.

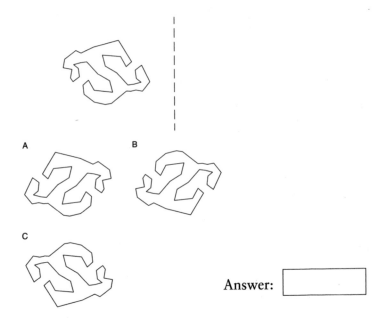

Answer: [   ]

Q2.

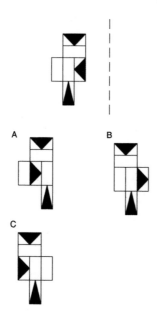

Answer: [   ]

Q3.

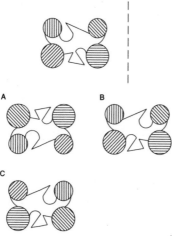

Answer: [   ]

Q4.

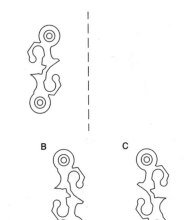

Answer: [   ]

Q5.

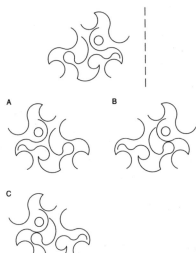

Answer: [   ]

End of test

Mini-test 8

Identify the mirror image of the question shape (reject any suggested answer in which any change other than reflection has occurred).

Q1.

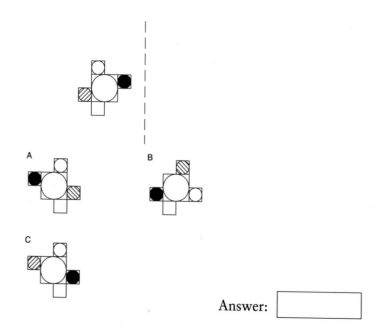

Answer: [   ]

Q2.

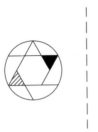

A

B

C

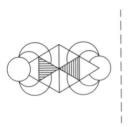

Answer: [   ]

Q3.

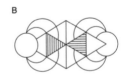

A

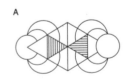

B

C

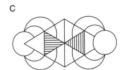

Answer: [   ]

Q4.

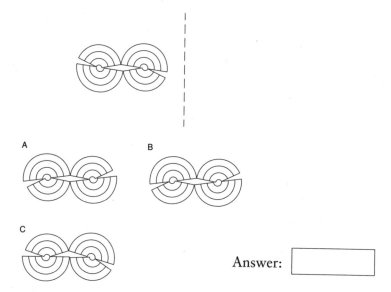

Answer: [   ]

Q5.

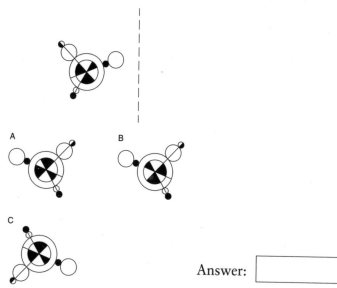

Answer: [   ]

End of test

Mini-test 9

Identify the answer shape, which has been rotated but is otherwise the same as the question shape.

Q1.

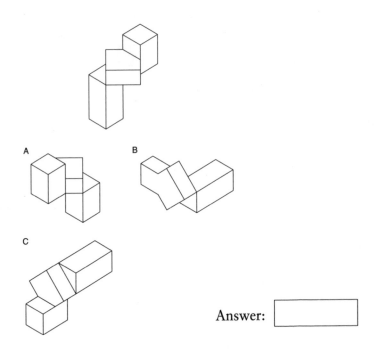

Answer: [   ]

Q2.

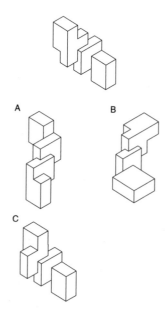

Answer: [ ]

Q3.

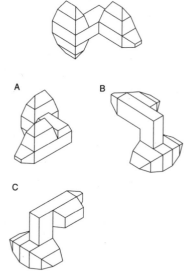

Answer: [ ]

Q4.

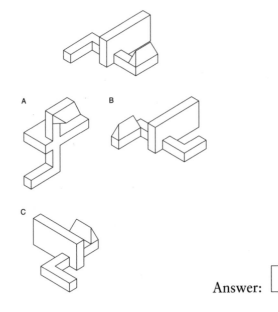

Answer:

Q5.

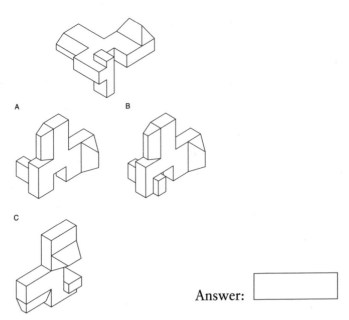

Answer:

End of test

Mini-test 10

Identify the answer shape, which has been rotated but is otherwise the same as the question shape.

Q1.

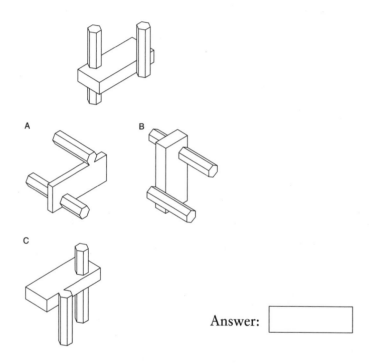

Answer: [   ]

Q2.

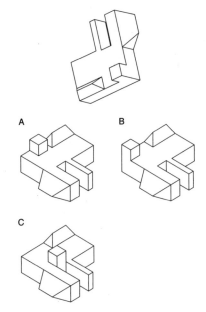

Answer:

Q3.

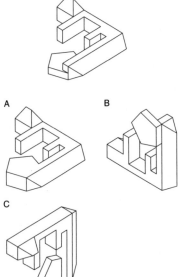

Answer:

Q4.

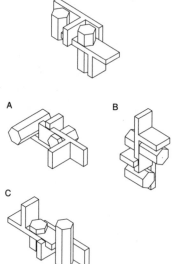

A   B

C

Answer: _____

Q5.

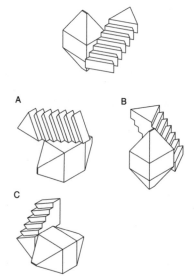

A   B

C

Answer: _____

End of test

Answers and explanations

Chapter 2 Abstract reasoning

Chapter 2, Style one

Q1. Answer: C
Explanation: The features in common are an odd number of triangles, the majority of which are shaded.

Q2. Answer: A
Explanation: Both question shapes are constructed from two triangles, in one shape inside a circle and in the other shape outside a circle. Only suggested answer A conforms to this, by having two triangles inside a circle. B has one triangle inside and another outside a circle. C has one triangle and two circles.

Q3. Answer: A
Explanation: The question shapes and A comprise one circle, three triangles and five squares (four of which are shaded).

Q4. Answer: C
Explanation: The four designs that make up the question shapes are moving in a clockwise direction. In suggested answer C the four shapes are in the correct position should they move in a clockwise direction once more.

Q5. Answer: C
Explanation: The question shapes include a sequence that runs diamond, square, circle, triangle. This sequence is correctly replicated only in suggested answer C.

Q6. Answer: A
Explanation: Both question shapes contain an odd number of shapes, and only suggested answer A shares this quality.

Q7. Answer: C
Explanation: The two question shapes contain respectively 18 and 12 dots, a difference of 6. If you add 6 to 18 you get 24, the number of dots found in suggested answer C.

Q8. Answer: C
Explanation: The question shapes are both quadrilaterals, as is suggested answer C.

Q9. Answer: B
Explanation: Both question shapes start with a shaded circle at their top, as does suggested answer B.

Q10. Answer: C
Explanation: In the case of both question shapes the number of sides and curved lines within them correspond.

Chapter 2, Style two

Q11. Answer: C
Explanation: The outer small circle is moving in a clockwise direction around the outside of the large circle.

Q12. Answer: A
Explanation: Notice that the squares making up the question are numbered and that the empty box is number 3. Notice also that the square becomes a triangle (pointing downwards) and then turns back into a square and that the direction of the arrow is alternating: in 1 and 3 it is pointing downwards and in 2 and 4 it is pointing upwards.

Q13. Answer: A
Explanation: In this sort of question you must treat the shaded shape as something that moves around in either a clockwise or an anticlockwise direction, obscuring the shapes underneath. In this example the shaded shape is rotating in a clockwise direction. Its starting position therefore is over the triangle.

Q14. Answer: A
Explanation: The question shapes comprise: two squares and two circles; the gap; another two squares and two circles; and four squares. Given the suggested answers, A is the best choice, as it then creates a series that runs: two squares and two circles; four circles; two squares and two circles; four squares.

Q15. Answer: B
Explanation: The series starts from the bottom left and moves in an anticlockwise direction. At each step in the series one of the small circles is transformed into a spike. The series starts with four small circles and ends with four spikes.

Q16. Answer: A
Explanation: The number of shaded squares is decreasing by three each step. The series starts with nine shaded squares and decreases to six, then three and finally no shaded squares.

Q17. Answer: C
Explanation: A shape is removed each step, and the direction of the shading in the shapes is moving in a clockwise direction. So the circle is shaded first diagonally, then horizontally, then diagonally again and finally vertically.

Q18. Answer: B
Explanation: At each step in the series an extra circle is shaded and a cross removed. Also the direction of the line of circles is alternating from top left to top right. B is the correct suggested answer because the line of circles starts top left.

Q19. Answer: A
Explanation: A circle is changed into two arrow heads at each step in the series, and the direction of the arrows is alternating.

Q20. Answer: A
Explanation: Notice the large capital 'L' shape in the diagram. It is rotating in a clockwise direction within the shape. The diamonds are changing into squares and back again (alternating).

Q21. Answer: C
Explanation: Again this question involves a large capital 'L' shape, but it is partly obscured by other shapes at some points while it rotates in an anticlockwise direction.

Q22. Answer: C
Explanation: In this series the empty segment is in fact covering the shape below, and as it rotates around the circle in a clockwise direction it covers another shape and reveals the shapes that it had previously covered.

Q23. Answer: B
Explanation: In each step of the sequence four triangles are transformed into one square.

Q24. Answer: B
Explanation: At each step shapes are transformed. The changes start with the squares, which two at a time become circles, and when all these have been transformed it is the turn of the triangles, which become diamonds.

Q25. Answer: A
Explanation: The series of crosses counts down 3, 2, 1 and then starts again.

Q26. Answer: B
Explanation: The shapes are alternating between squares and octagons, and the number of crosses represents the 7 times table: $7 \times 0 = 0, 7 \times 1 = 7, 7 \times 2 = 14, 7 \times 3 = 21$.

Q27. Answer: C
Explanation: The number of randomly placed and shaped triangles is increasing by two each step.

Q28. Answer: C
Explanation: Squares are transformed into moons, and then as the series progresses circles are transformed into triangles. The side of the diagram that is shaded is alternating from left to right and between two and three shaded shapes.

Q29. Answer: A
Explanation: The wavy lines are decreasing by two each step in the series, and the number of small lines arranged in a circle is increasing by three each step.

Q30. Answer: B
Explanation: If you count the number of sides that make up all the shapes in each step of the series you will realize that they are increasing by five each step.

Q31. Answer: A
Explanation: A circle becomes a triangle and a square becomes a shaded circle each step in the sequence.

Q32. Answer: C
Explanation: The shaded boxes form a line diagonally across the squares, and at each step in the series this line moves up to the top of the squares and then starts again at the bottom right-hand corner.

Q33. Answer: B
Explanation: The shapes represent the series 3, 2, 1, which is repeated: 3, 2, 1, 3.

Q34. Answer: A
Explanation: At each step, shapes are transformed: egg timers become diamonds, circles become squares and triangles become crosses. The triangles/crosses and egg timers/diamonds also change position, alternating from top to bottom. (The circles and squares remain in the middle.)

Q35. Answer: A
Explanation: The shaded segment of the square in the middle of the shape is rotating clockwise, while the randomly placed black marks numbering 2, 3, 4 and 5 are rotating clockwise.

Chapter 2, Style three

Q36. Answer: C
Explanation: The shape is rotating anticlockwise, but the shaded area remains at the top and the shaded segment of the centre of the shape is alternating.

Q37. Answer: A
Explanation: At each step the shape at the top of the previous diagram moves into the box and the shape at the bottom takes its place.

Q38. Answer: D
Explanation: The type of shapes is irrelevant to the question, and the number of shapes is increased by one each step of the series.

Q39. Answer: B
Explanation: The number of lines from which each shape is constructed is following the sequence 4, 3, 2, 1 and then 4 again.

Q40. Answer: C
Explanation: The shape is first pressed completely flat vertically and then stretched horizontally until it forms a line.

Q41. Answer: A
Explanation: The arrow is being rotated in an anticlockwise direction. First it is rotated 360 degrees (this is why it appears the same between steps 1 and 2), then 180 degrees, then 90 degrees and finally 45 degrees.

Q42. Answer: A
Explanation: At each step the number of shapes increases by one, and the number of sides that the shapes have decreases by two.

Q43. Answer: C
Explanation: The shapes are rotating 90 degrees in a clockwise direction each step of the series. Notice that suggested answer B is wrong because the base of the triangle is on the wrong side.

Q44. Answer: B
Explanation: The circles are moved across the shape and the number of boxes is changing but the solution relates to the total number of circles which is consistantly five and only suggested answer B also contains five circles.

Q45. Answer: A
Explanation: The background shading is increasing from none to a quarter to a half and finally to all shaded; the shapes are also alternating between circles and arrows, and the direction of the arrows and the position of the dots in the circles are also alternating between the top and bottom.

Q46. Answer: B
Explanation: The shapes are made up from overlying circles, triangles and squares. The sequence begins with the order circle, triangle, square, then moves to triangle, square, circle and then

square, circle, triangle, etc. The fifth step in the series is triangle, square, circle. The answers are made up of the same shapes, but instead of being overlapping they are arranged in a row. Suggested answer B offers the same sequence of shapes as the fifth step in the sequence.

Q47. Answer: B
Explanation: The outer shapes of the first two steps are a semi-complete and a complete square – a four-sided shape. The next two steps are a semi-complete and a complete three-sided shape. The next shape in the series therefore would be a semi-complete two-sided shape. The inner shapes alternate complete and incomplete, and in the next step of the series it is the turn of the complete shape.

Q48. Answer: C
Explanation: Starting with 1, the series of shapes represents the sequence add 3 (=4), minus 2 (=2), add 1 (=3), minus 0 (=3).

Q49. Answer: D
Explanation: The direction of the shading is irrelevant to the question. The series starts with an unshaded square overlaid by an unshaded circle and shaded square; then there is a shaded square overlaid by an unshaded circle and shaded square, and then a shaded square, circle and square. The only combination not included in the series is all three shapes unshaded, which is found in suggested answer D.

Q50. Answer: A
Explanation: The shape is rotating anticlockwise 90 degrees each step in the series.

Q51. Answer: A
Explanation: The number of sides to the shapes follows the sequence 3 + 1 = 4 + 2 = 6. The next step in the sequence is 6 + 3 = 9, which is represented as 9 circles in suggested answer A.

Q52. Answer: B
Explanation: The shape is rotated 90 degrees clockwise each step in the series.

Q53. Answer: B
Explanation: Each step represents a fraction (for example, 3 circles over 6 triangles = 3/6). If you cancel the fractions down you get the sequence 1/2, 1/4, 1/8, and the next step is 1/16.

Q54. Answer: C
Explanation: The shapes portray a pentagon overlying an arrow that is moving downwards. In the last step of the series the hexagon has been removed, and by studying previous diagrams you are able to estimate the dimensions of the arrow correctly as in suggested answer C.

Q55. Answer: D
Explanation: The series follows the sequence 1, 2, 3, 2. You can make sense of this as 1 + 2 = 3 + 2 = 5, so the correct answer is suggested answer D with five shapes.

Q56. Answer: D
Explanation: At each step the number of circles decreases by two (from 6 to 0), and the number of triangles increases by four from 0 to 12. The direction of the triangles alternates, and the shapes alternate top and bottom.

Q57. Answer: C
Explanation: The order of the shapes – triangle top, then shaded circle and square – is repeated in the next step as if they were placed in the same order but one on top of the other. The order of the shapes in the third step is correctly represented by suggested answer C (note the triangle would be obscured by the square).

Q58. Answer: B
Explanation: In the first step of the series four triangles point towards each other. In the second step three triangles point

towards each other and one points away. In the third step two triangles point towards each other. So suggested answer B correctly completes the series, as all four point away from each other.

Q59. Answer: B
Explanation: The number of flat surfaces in the shape is decreasing by three each step in the series, beginning with nine. The final shape in the series would have no flat surfaces.

Q60. Answer: C
Explanation: At each step in the series the shape is rotated clockwise by 90 degrees.

Chapter 2, Style four

Q61. Answer: CD
Explanation: The code for a quadrilateral is B and for vertical lines E. The code for a 10-sided figure is C and for diagonal lines D.

Q62. Answer: AA
Explanation: The code for an empty half of the shape is A (one dot C, two D and three Y).

Q63. Answer: YEN
Explanation: The code for no shading is N and for a shape with shading M. A partially obscured pentagon is D and one not obscured is E. The code for a circle is X, for a square Y and for a triangle Z.

Q64. Answer: BNP
Explanation: When there are three shapes in a column the shape is coded B and when not in a column C. If the shape is framed (with a triangle or square) it is coded M, and if it has no frame N. If one shape is shaded, the code P is applied; if three shapes are shaded, code Y is used.

Q65. Answer: XAP
Explanation: The code for a single triangle is X and for three shapes or more P. A shaded semicircle is signified by the letter A.

Q66. Answer: MZ
Explanation: A circle containing two other shapes (alongside each other) is signified with the letter M. A circle containing a shape that also contains a shape is coded with an N. The code for four triangles (in either the rectangle or the circle) is Z. The code for three triangles is X.

Q67. Answer: DP
Explanation: An elongated circle is coded with a C. Three segments created by the overlapping circles are coded with an R. Four segments are coded P. Shading is coded with a D and no shading Z.

Q68. Answer: DR
Explanation: An odd number of circles is coded with a P and an even number with a D. An odd number of triangles is coded with an E and an even number with an R.

Q69. Answer: AC
Explanation: A six-sided figure is coded with an A and a five-sided figure with a B. A large circle is coded with a C and a small circle with a D.

Q70. Answer: C
Explanation: A shape containing two points facing right is coded with a B, and a shape containing two points facing left is coded with a C.

Q71. Answer: BP
Explanation: A shape with one sloping side is signified with a D and two with a B. Shading of any style is coded P and no shading Q.

Q72. Answer: SZ
Explanation: A complete shape is signified with an S and an incomplete shape (the sphere – an incomplete circle – and cube) with an R. T signifies a three-dimensional object and Z a shape with straight sides.

Q73. Answer: ADQ
Explanation: Shading from left to right is signified with the letter A and vertical shading with B. A shape with four inner designs is coded with a P, and a shape that does not have four inner designs is coded with a Q. If the outermost shape is shaded it is coded with a C, and if it is not shaded it is coded with a D.

Q74. Answer: TYE
Explanation: An S signifies an odd number of irregular rectangles or circles; an even number is coded with a T. If the circles contained within the squares are consistently one side or the other then the code is X; if they alternate from side to side the code is Y. A four-sided framing shape is signified with a D, a five-sided frame with an E and a three-sided frame with an F.

Q75. Answer: CX
Explanation: A shape containing a full blackened segment is coded with an X, wavy shading is coded with a D, vertical shading is coded with a C and horizontal shading is coded with a Y.

Q76. Answer: PR
Explanation: Two triangles are coded with P and one triangle with Q. If a large triangle is found in the shape then it is given the code R; otherwise it is given the code M.

Q77. Answer: WN
Explanation: Five shapes are signified with the letter Y. All but one shape shaded is signified with an M. Four shapes are signified with a W, and three without shading with an N.

Q78. Answer: PA
Explanation: Three shapes are coded with a P and two shapes with a Q. One shaded triangle is coded with an A, and no shading is coded with a B.

Q79. Answer: MT
Explanation: A shape containing wavy lines is coded with an N, while a shape with no wavy lines is coded with an M. A shape comprising five shapes is coded with a Q, and a shape comprising six shapes is coded with a T.

Q80. Answer: B
Explanation: An eight-sided figure is signified with the letter A, and a four-sided figure with the letter B. If the shape has a hole it is signified with an X.

Q81. Answer: EPX
Explanation: If there are horizontal lines then they are signified by an X. If the total number of lines is an odd number, the shape is coded P, and if an even number it is coded Q. If the number of vertical lines is an odd number this is signified with a G, and if an even number it is signified with an E.

Q82. Answer: BD
Explanation: A partially obscured triangle is signified by the letter B, and two rectangles are represented by the letter D. Whether or not the triangle is shaded is irrelevant to the question.

Q83. Answer: NQ
Explanation: Four shaded circles are coded with a P, and a shape containing a triangle or triangles with an N. If all the circles are shaded then the shape is coded with a Q.

Q84. Answer: PD
Explanation: A shape containing one or more small shapes is signified by a P, and a total of two shapes by a D.

Q85. Answer: BC
Explanation: A single line in any shape is signified with the letter A, and two lines with a B. One more small shape than the number of lines is signified with a C.

Chapter 2, Four mini-tests

Chapter 2, Mini-test 1

Q1. Answer: A
Explanation: Both question shapes contain two circles, as do suggested answers A and C, but only suggested answer A also shares the quality with the question shapes that one of its shapes touches the outer edge of the square containing the shapes.

Q2. Answer: A
Explanation: Half the number of shapes making up the question shapes are shaded, as is the case in suggested answer A.

Q3. Answer: D
Explanation: The dots on the shapes follow the sequence of the first six prime numbers: 2, 3, 5, 7, 11, 13 (this is a sequence that you should learn to recognize if you do not already know it).

Q4. Answer: C
Explanation: Both question shapes have the same number of shapes inside them as they have sides and have the same number of shaded shapes as they have sides. All the suggested answers have only one set of shapes, some of which are shaded, and only suggested answer C has the same number of shapes and shaded shapes as sides.

Q5. Answer: B
Explanation: The sum of the shapes making up both question shapes is a multiple of 3, and only suggested answer B is also made up of a sum of shapes that is a multiple of 3.

Chapter 2, Mini-test 2

Q1. Answer: D
Explanation: At each step in the series the small circle is migrating downwards and the line upwards.

Q2. Answer: A
Explanation: Arrows become squares and change back, the three circles become a small triangle and change back, diamonds alternate in size, and the large triangle appears in the second and fourth steps rotated 180 degrees.

Q3. Answer: B
Explanation: The clock shape (displaying 3 o'clock) is rotated first 360 degrees, then 180 degrees and finally 90 degrees.

Q4. Answer: D
Explanation: The series of shapes is made from right-angled and equilateral triangles, and the shading follows the sequence one right-angled triangle and one equilateral triangle (box 2), two right-angled triangles (box 3), one right-angled triangle and one equilateral triangle (box 4) and then two equilateral triangles (box 1).

Q5. Answer: C
Explanation: The dots on the pole increase by three each step in the series, from 2 to 5, 8 and 11. The shapes on the top of the pole form the four possible combinations when the bases of the triangles remain horizontal.

Chapter 2, Mini-test 3

Q1. Answer: D
Explanation: The shape at the bottom of the previous step moves into the circle, and the shape at the top in the previous shape moves to the bottom.

Q2. Answer: A
Explanation: At each step in the sequence the operation alternates from plus to minus and follows the sequence $4 + 1 = 5, - 2 = 3, + 3 = 6, - 4 = 2$.

Q3. Answer: B
Explanation: At each step the shape is rotating 90 degrees.

Q4. Answer: C
Explanation: In the first shape the triangle overlies the circle and then the circle overlies the triangle. In the third step the triangle again overlies the circle; only now it points upwards. In the next step of the sequence you would expect the circle to overlie the triangle and, given its new position, the circle would obscure the triangle. This means that the correct representation of the shape is shown at C.

Q5. Answer: D
Explanation: At first sight the answer would appear to be a shape divided into five, but there are two suggested answers divided this way. If you count the lines making the shapes then you might expect the answer to have seven sides, but three suggested answers have this quality. The answer is both the number of ways the shape is divided and the number of sides. In the first shape there are 4 sides and 2 divisions, in the second shape there are 5 sides and 3 divisions, and in the third shape there are 6 sides and 4 divisions. The next step therefore is a shape with 7 sides and 5 divisions, and only answer D offers this combination.

Chapter 2, Mini-test 4

Q1. Answer: CD
Explanation: A circle or two semicircles are represented with the letter A. Two circles or a circle and two semicircles are represented by a C. A square is represented by a D.

Q2. Answer: R
Explanation: Counting the sides of the internal shape including those formed by the shaded area it is found that P = 4 and R = 5 (O = 6).

Q3. Answer: BA
Explanation: Counting the number of short lines making up the outer and inner shapes it is found that 12 = A, 14 = B and 9 = C. The question shape is made up of 14 short lines forming the outer square and 12 lines forming the arrow.

Q4. Answer: EF
Explanation: A shape made from five items is signified with the letter G. If all the items are curved or circular this is signified with the letter D. A shape that is made of three items is coded F. A shape that is made of triangles is coded E.

Q5. Answer: CA
Explanation: One circle is signified with a C and two with a B. A partially obscured rectangle is signified with the letter A; if it is not obscured it is signified with a D.

Chapter 3 Input-type diagrammatic reasoning

Chapter 3, Type 1

Q1. Answer: D
Explanation: The first change deletes the K, next the U is changed to V and finally a P is inserted between the Z and the L.

Q2. Answer: A
Explanation: The first change deletes the P, then the N is replaced with an M and finally the C and the first M are exchanged.

Q3. Answer: C
Explanation: The A becomes B, then the sequence is reversed to become RDEGBUG and finally the B becomes a C.

Q4. Answer: B
Explanation: First the S is deleted, then a P is inserted between the A and the first T and finally we replace the first T with a U.

Q5. Answer: C
Explanation: The first rule deletes the E, then the second I is replaced with a J and finally the sequence is reversed to read DJTION.

Q6. Answer: A
Explanation: First the I is deleted, then the sequence is reversed to read PASSNG, next the first S becomes a T and finally the N is replaced with an O.

Q7. Answer: A
Explanation: First exchange the E with the last letter T, then insert a P between the G and the second T, next change the G into an H and finally delete the E.

Q8. Answer: B
Explanation: First reverse the sequence to read SCHINA, then change the C into a B, then insert a P between the H and the I and finally delete the A.

Q9. Answer: D
Explanation: First replace the O with P and then the S with T, next exchange the first T and last P to give PTPHTT and finally delete the second P.

Q10. Answer: C
Explanation: First reverse the sequence to read AJMUCCR, then insert a P between the M and the U, next replace the J with an I and finally reverse the sequence again to read RCCUPMIA.

Chapter 3, Type 2

Q11. Answer: B

Q12. Answer: D

Q13. Answer: C

Q14. Answer: A

Q15. Answer: C

Q16. Answer: B

Q17. Answer: D

Q18. Answer: B

Q19. Answer: A

Q20. Answer: C

Chapter 3, Type 3

Q21. Answer: B

Q22. Answer: D

Q23. Answer: C

Q24. Answer: A

Q25. Answer: C

Q26. Answer: A

Q27. Answer: D

Q28. Answer: B

Q29. Answer: C

Q30. Answer: A

Chapter 3, Type 4

Q31. Answer: D

Q32. Answer: B

Q33. Answer: C

Q34. Answer: A

Q35. Answer: D

Q36. Answer: B

Q37. Answer: C

Q38. Answer: C

Q39. Answer: A

Q40. Answer: C

Chapter 3, Twelve mini-tests

Chapter 3, Mini-test 1
Q1. Answer: A
Explanation: First replace the L with an X, then switch the U and V and finally reverse the sequence to obtain XKGFEUV.

Q2. Answer: D
Explanation: First reverse the sequence to read ENINNET, then exchange the middle N and the T (which has become the final character) and finally insert SA.

Q3. Answer: B
Explanation: First we switch the I and the second A to make ZAALITER, then switch the Z and the first A, next replace the first letter with a B.

Q4. Answer: B
Explanation: First switch the second and fifth characters to read FDREIRI, then insert SA between the sixth and seventh characters, then reverse the characters and finally switch the first and second letters to give you AISRIERDF.

Q5. Answer: B
Explanation: First replace the middle character M with C, then replace the first letter with B, then exchange the D with the C and finally replace the last character, C, with X.

Chapter 3, Mini-test 2

Q1. Answer: C
Explanation: First replace the third letter with the number 3 (note the command is to replace the third letter, not the third item, so we replace the W), next replace the V with the number 7 and finally replace the B with the number 9.

Q2. Answer: B
Explanation: First delete the third item to get WNK999R, then replace the first number with Z and finally replace the fourth item (the Z) with the letters WR.

Q3. Answer: D
Explanation: First replace the C with B, then replace the L with the number 3, next replace the last item (and fifth letter) with the number 7 and finally replace the 4 with the letters WR.

Q4. Answer: A
Explanation: First replace the fifth letter, E, with the number 7, then replace the first letter, A, with the number 9, next delete the third item and finally replace the last letter with the previous one in the alphabet to read 925N7C7.

Q5. Answer: A
Explanation: First replace the third letter with the number 3 (note that the second letter is I, not the number 1), then delete the H (the third item), next replace the fourth item with the letters WR and finally replace the first number with Z to read Z5WR3B83.

Chapter 3, Mini-test 3

Q1. Answer: B
Explanation: First change the third letter to lower case, then change the first letter to lower case and finally replace the second number with an upper-case P.

Q2. Answer: C
Explanation: First replace the fourth lower-case letter with the next in the alphabet, next replace the second number with an upper-case P and finally replace the second lower-case letter with the next in the alphabet.

Q3. Answer: D
Explanation: First insert the letters Nr to create the sequence iNrnter555MAR, next exchange the first and last items and finally exchange the second and sixth items.

Q4. Answer: A
Explanation: First change the third letter (the T) to lower case, then exchange the second and sixth items, next change the first letter to lower case and finally exchange the first and last items.

Q5. Answer: C
Explanation: First replace the fourth lower-case letter with the next in the alphabet, next replace the second number with an upper-case P, then exchange the first and last characters and finally replace the second lower-case letter with the next in the alphabet to give the sequence sST6PdhaU.

Chapter 3, Mini-test 4
Q1. Answer: D

Q2. Answer: A

Q3. Answer: B

Q4. Answer: D

Q5. Answer: D

Chapter 3, Mini-test 5
Q1. Answer: B

Q2. Answer: D

Q3. Answer: C

Q4. Answer: A

Q5. Answer: B

Chapter 3, Mini-test 6
Q1. Answer: A

Q2. Answer: D

Q3. Answer: B

Q4. Answer: C

Q5. Answer: C

Chapter 3, Mini-test 7
Q1. Answer: C

Q2. Answer: A

Q3. Answer: D

Q4. Answer: B

Q5. Answer: B

Chapter 3, Mini-test 8
Q1. Answer: C

Q2. Answer: A

Q3. Answer: A

Q4. Answer: B

Q5. Answer: D

Chapter 3, Mini-test 9
Q1. Answer: B

Q2. Answer: B

Q3. Answer: D

Q4. Answer: C

Q5. Answer: B

Chapter 3, Mini-test 10
Q1. Answer: C

Q2. Answer: A

Q3. Answer: C

Q4. Answer: D

Q5. Answer: C

Chapter 3, Mini-test 11
Q1. Answer: D

Q2. Answer: B

Q3. Answer: A

Q4. Answer: C

Q5. Answer: D

Chapter 3, Mini-test 12

Q1. Answer: B

Q2. Answer: C

Q3. Answer: D

Q4. Answer: A

Q5. Answer: D

Chapter 4 Conceptual or spatial reasoning

Chapter 4, Type 1

Q1. Answer: c)
Explanation: a) has the wrong sequence of squares and rectangles, b) has only squares and d) has too many sides.

Q2. Answer: b)
Explanation: The cube has six sides; a) has only five, while d) has seven, and c) has different rectangular forms.

Q3. Answer: a)
Explanation: In b) you fold the right sides one over the other, while the left side is missing, c) has different geometric forms, and in d) the depth is missing.

Q4. Answer: c)
Explanation: a) has the top twice, b) has different geometric forms, and in d) the top is missing.

Q5. Answer: c)
Explanation: In a) the position of the 'houses' is wrong, b) has different geometric forms, and d) has too many sides.

Q6. Answer: a)
Explanation: a) is the only solution with a square as the base and four equal triangles.

Q7. Answer: b)
Explanation: In a) the triangles would need to be rotated, c) does not have a triangle base, and d) has too many sides.

Q8. Answer: d)
Explanation: The form has only two sides that are not rectangles; a) has four, b) has different geometric forms, and c) has the not-rectangle forms in the wrong place.

Q9. Answer: a)
Explanation: In b) the back is too short, c) has different geometric forms, and d) has too many sides.

Q10. Answer: b)
Explanation: a) has too many sides, in c) the left side has been reflected and does not fit any more, and in d) the downward-looking shape has been reflected.

Chapter 4, Type 2

Q11. Answer: c)
Explanation: a) shows the right side, and b) shows the left side.

Q12. Answer: c)
Explanation: a) shows the left side, and b) shows the right side.

Q13. Answer: a)
Explanation: In b) the middle part is too long, and c) has too many edges (count them and compare with the original).

Q14. Answer: b)
Explanation: a) shows the right side, and c) shows the left side.

Q15. Answer: a)
Explanation: All you can see from above is the three steps; in b) this zigzag form is not part of the original, and c) shows the right side.

Q16. Answer: c)
Explanation: The rounded cover of the little box is just a plain rectangle from above; a) shows the elevation of the box that you cannot see from above, but only from the side, and b) shows the half-moon that you cannot see from above.

Q17. Answer: b)
Explanation: The tubes are cut straight, and you cannot see the openings as suggested in a); c) does not consider that the tubes are piled up.

Q18. Answer: b)
Explanation: If you see a pyramid from the side it looks like a triangle, so a) is not correct, and c) shows a cone rather than a pyramid on the top of the cube.

Q19. Answer: c)
Explanation: a) shows a form with an additional cube in the corner, and in b) the sides of the 'L' are too long.

Q20. Answer: a)
Explanation: The sloped elements are exactly as long as the cubes from above, even though the slope itself is longer, which is shown in b); from above you cannot see the sides of the sloped elements as suggested in c).

Chapter 4, Type 3

Q21. Answer: a)
Explanation: The long side of the triangle should be along the mirror line; b) is the same shape as the original, and c) is the mirror image but in the other direction.

Q22. Answer: c)
Explanation: a) has been mirrored in the other direction, and b) is the same as the original.

Q23. Answer: c)
Explanation: a) is a modified shape, and b) is the same as the original.

Q24. Answer: b)
Explanation: In a) and c) some 'holes' have been moved.

Q25. Answer: c)
Explanation: a) has been rotated, and b) has been reflected vertically.

Q26. Answer: b)
Explanation: a) has the right shape, but the shadings are in different sectors, and c) has the small hexagon in a wrong position.

Q27. Answer: a)
Explanation: b) has been rotated, and c) has been reflected and rotated.

Q28. Answer: a)
Explanation: b) and c) are both rotations of the original.

Q29. Answer: b)
Explanation: a) has the right shape, but the shadings are in different sectors, and c) mirrors only the diagonal line in the central rectangle, while the rest is the same as the original.

Q30. Answer: b)
Explanation: In a) the horizontal axis has not been reflected, while the vertical axis has been rotated, and in c) the horizontal axis has not been reflected.

Chapter 4, Type 4

Q31. Answer: b)
Explanation: In a) the small 'roof' shape has been moved, in c) the small 'roof' shape is missing, and in d) the central part of the shape is too small.

Q32. Answer: a)
Explanation: b) is wrong because it represents an extruded irregular quadrangle, in c) the shape has been shortened, and in d) the shape has been lengthened.

Q33. Answer: d)
Explanation: In a), b) and c) the rectangular shape has been moved.

Q34. Answer: b)
Explanation: It is the only one with a 'roof' on the intersection of the 'L' shape.

Q35. Answer: a)
Explanation: b) has a 'W' shape instead of a 'T' shape, and c) has a 'Z' shape instead of a 'T' shape.

Q36. Answer: a)
Explanation: In b) the small cube has been moved to the opposite side of the truncated pyramid, and in c) the small cube has been truncated.

Q37. Answer: a)
Explanation: In b) the thin triangle has been moved upwards, and in c) the thin triangle has been moved downwards.

Q38. Answer: a)
Explanation: In b) the small cube has been moved, and in c) the irregular shape has been shortened.

Q39. Answer: c)
Explanation: In a) and b) the small parallelepiped beside the 'roof' shape has been deformed.

Q40. Answer: b)
Explanation: In a) and c) the small parallelepiped has been moved.

Chapter 4, Type 5

Q41. Answer: c)
Explanation: In a) the triangular shape has been deformed, and in b) and d) the cube has been deformed.

Q42. Answer: d)
Explanation: In a) the big triangular shape has been thickened, in b) the big triangular shape has been thinned, and in c) the small triangular shape has been deformed.

Q43. Answer: b)
Explanation: In a) and c) the right triangular shape has been truncated, and in d) both triangular shapes have had the edges cut off.

Q44. Answer: b)
Explanation: In a) and c) the small box has been moved.

Q45. Answer: a)
Explanation: In b) and c) the hexagonal shape has been deformed.

Q46. Answer: a)
Explanation: In b) both shapes are different, and in c) the right shape has been modified.

Q47. Answer: a)
Explanation: In b) the semicircular shape is missing, and in c) the small triangular shape has been enlarged.

Q48. Answer: c)
Explanation: In a) and b) the small cube on the left shape has been moved.

Q49. Answer: b)
Explanation: In a) the rhomb has been truncated, and in c) the 'roof' shape has been truncated.

Q50. Answer: a)
Explanation: In b) the right face of the fourth layer (counting from the top) is too short, and in c) the right face of the third layer (counting from the top) is too long.

Chapter 4, Ten mini-tests

Chapter 4, Mini-test 1

Q1. Answer: a)
Explanation: b) and c) have one of the L shapes in the wrong position.

Q2. Answer: b)
Explanation: b) is the only one with the right number of squares; you need only five, because the top is made from the triangles.

Q3. Answer: c)
Explanation: In a) the long rectangle that covers the volume is in a wrong position, and in b) there is a wrong geometric form.

Q4. Answer: b)
Explanation: In a) the sides of the 'T' are double, and in c) the closure on the top of the shape is missing.

Hint: A quick method to see if an answer is valid is to check the number of surfaces of the figure and compare it to the surfaces given in the unfolded shape.

Q5. Answer: b)
Explanation: In a) the right side is double, and in c) the depth of the figure is missing.

Chapter 4, Mini-test 2

Q1. Answer: a)
Explanation: In b) the cover of the sloped side is double, and c) has not enough surfaces.

Q2. Answer: c)
Explanation: a) has not enough surfaces, and in b) the rectangle that gives the depth to the form is in a wrong position.

Q3. Answer: a)
Explanation: In b) the little squares that form the cube are in the wrong position, and c) has one of the little squares in a wrong position.

Q4. Answer: b)
Explanation: a) shows a different form with regular sides, and in c) the big triangles are too long.

Q5. Answer: b)
Explanation: In a) the little squares are in the wrong position, and c) does not have enough surfaces.

Chapter 4, Mini-test 3

Q1. Answer: a)
Explanation: In b) the underneath 'W' is the mirror image of the correct shape, and in c) the 'W' has been transformed.

Q2. Answer: b)
Explanation: a) has not enough surfaces, and in c) the underneath 'U' is the mirror image of the correct shape.

Q3. Answer: a)
Explanation: In b) there are too many squares and the triangles are on a wrong segment, and in c) the triangles are on a wrong segment.

Q4. Answer: a)
Explanation: b) has too many rectangles, and in c) the underneath form is the mirror image of the correct shape.

Q5. Answer: a)
Explanation: In b) the small squares are in the wrong position, and in c) the small squares underneath are in the wrong position.

Chapter 4, Mini-test 4

Q1. Answer: b)
Explanation: In a) the outer square is in the wrong position, in c) there are too many squares.

Q2. Answer: a)
Explanation: In b) the half-moons are in the wrong position and there are not enough squares, and in c) there are not enough of them.

Q3. Answer: b)
Explanation: The shape is made from two pentagons; in a) one pentagon is missing, and in c) the number is right but in this configuration you don't get the right form if you fold them.

Q4. Answer: c)
Explanation: In a) four of the triangles are in the wrong position and do not allow the figure to be closed, and in b) there are not enough triangles (only 18 instead of 20) and the folded figure would be irregular.

Q5. Answer: b)
Explanation: The form is made from six squares and eight triangles; in a) there are not enough squares and some triangles are in the wrong position, and in c) there are too many squares.

Chapter 4, Mini-test 5

Q1. Answer: a)
Explanation: b) and d) have no rectangles, and c) has no big square.

Q2. Answer: c)
Explanation: In a) the long triangles are not equal, in b) all the triangles have equal sides, and in d) there are rectangles in the unfolded shape.

Q3. Answer: b)
Explanation: a) is too thick, in c) the triangles are incorrect because they have three equal sides, and in d) the triangles are again wrong, because they have no equal sides.

Q4. Answer: b)
Explanation: a) and c) have only two triangular shapes.

Q5. Answer: c)
Explanation: a) has incorrect trapezoidal sides, and b) lacks a small rectangle.

Chapter 4, Mini-test 6

Q1. Answer: a)
Explanation: a) is correct because it is the only suggested answer with a small square.

Q2. Answer: c)
Explanation: a) has three squares, and b) has eight triangles.

Q3. Answer: b)
Explanation: a) is wrong because it has four slim rectangles, and c) has no small squares.

Q4. Answer: b)
Explanation: a) lacks a slim rectangle, and c) has an incorrect 'L' shape.

Q5. Answer: c)
Explanation: a) has an incorrect 'T' shape, and b) has an incorrect 'W' shape.

Chapter 4, Mini-test 7

Q1. Answer: a)
Explanation: b) has been reflected vertically, and c) has been rotated.

Q2. Answer: c)
Explanation: a) is a modified shape, and in b) the central shading has been moved to the rectangle on the right side.

Q3. Answer: c)
Explanation: a) has been reflected vertically, and in b) the shadings in the circles have not been reflected.

Q4. Answer: c)
Explanation: a) is the same shape, and b) has been reflected vertically.

Q5. Answer: a)
Explanation: The other shapes are only partially reflected (some bits of the mirror image are represented in the original form).

Chapter 4, Mini-test 8

Q1. Answer: a)
Explanation: b) has the little squares and the shadings in different positions, and c) is the same as a) but the shadings have been inverted.

Q2. Answer: c)
Explanation: a) has been mirrored but also rotated, and b) is the same as c) but the shadings have been inverted.

Q3. Answer: a)
Explanation: In b) only the triangles with stripes have been reflected, and in c) the triangles with stripes have not been reflected.

Q4. Answer: b)
Explanation: In a) the left shape has been moved to the right and the right shape to the left and both have been slightly rotated, and in c) only the left shape has been reflected.

Q5. Answer: b)
Explanation: a) has the right shape but the shadings are in wrong sectors, and c) is a rotation.

Chapter 4, Mini-test 9

Q1. Answer: c)
Explanation: In a) and b) one of the parallelepipeds has been shortened.

Q2. Answer: a)
Explanation: In b) the small rectangular shape has been lengthened, and in c) the irregular shape has changed.

Q3. Answer: b)
Explanation: In a) a truncated 'roof' shape has been added to the central part of the figure, and in c) a small 'roof' shape has been removed.

Q4. Answer: c)
Explanation: a) has the roof upside down, and in b) the 'L' shape with the 'roof' has been reflected.

Q5. Answer: b)
Explanation: In a) the parallelepiped has been moved towards the opposite side of the 'roof' shape, and in c) the 'roof' shape has been moved.

Chapter 4, Mini-test 10

Q1. Answer: b)
Explanation: In a) the rectangular shape is too slim, and in c) one of the prisms has been moved.

Q2. Answer: b)
Explanation: In a) and c) the small cube has been moved.

Q3. Answer: c)
Explanation: In a) the pentagon has been thickened, and in b) the pentagon has been moved.

Q4. Answer: b)
Explanation: In a) and c) the two prisms have been inverted.

Q5. Answer: b)
Explanation: In a) the rectangular shape has been thickened, and in c) there is one 'step' missing.

T   s
ne   ce

You're
publis
indep
of boc
mana
educa
mind with some of the world's finest thinking.